LIFE
AFTER
DEATH

ROBERT L. MILLET

LIFE
AFTER
DEATH

INSIGHTS FROM LATTER-DAY REVELATION

DESERET BOOK COMPANY
SALT LAKE CITY, UTAH

Library of Congress Cataloging-in-Publication Data

Millet, Robert L.
    Life after death : insights from latter-day revelation / Robert L. Millet.
    p.   cm.
    Includes bibliographical references and index.
    ISBN 1-57345-541-5
    1. Future life—Church of Jesus Christ of Latter-day Saints.
  2. Church of Jesus Christ of Latter-day Saints—Doctrines. I. Title.
    BX8643.F87 M54 1999
    236.2'088283—dc21   99-15729
                                            CIP

Printed in the United States of America   72082-6482

10 9 8 7 6 5 4 3 2 1

CONTENTS

Prologue

In what some have called the post-Christian era, a time when men and women throughout the earth are leaving the faith of their parents and churches are closing down in an ever-increasing number, The Church of Jesus Christ of Latter-day Saints continues to grow in an unprecedented manner. What is it about our faith, the system of salvation commonly known as Mormonism, that has such appeal to people throughout the earth?

For one thing, many in our day are weary of the shifting sands of secularity and the ever-mobile standards of society. They long for a return to time-honored values and absolute truths. Because wickedness is widening, honest truth seekers yearn for something to hold on to, something of substance, something that will stand when all else is falling. At the same time, they long to be a part of a religious organization that requires something of them. In fact, recent sociological studies attest that the churches that grow are those that demand the most of their membership. For example, we as Latter-day Saints do not apologize for our position in regard to chastity and virtue, nor do we hesitate to teach the Word of Wisdom or the need to pay our tithes and offerings. We know that a person remains steadfast and immovable in the faith to the degree that he or she is invested in the faith.

More important than world conditions is the doctrine of

the LDS Church. It is comforting to know that God, our Heavenly Father, has a plan and there is purpose to struggles and suffering, even death. Our doctrine of a divine plan—including heaven and the hereafter—is especially appealing to those who encounter Mormonism. Two religious historians have written that "expressions of the eternal nature of love and the hope for heavenly reunion persist in contemporary Christianity." Yet, they assert, "hoping to meet one's family after death is a wish and not a theological argument. While most Christian clergy would not deny that wish, contemporary theologians are not interested in articulating the motif of meeting again in theological terms. The motifs of the modern heaven—eternal progress, love, and fluidity between earth and the other world—while acknowledged by pastors in their funeral sermons, are not fundamental to contemporary Christianity. Priests and pastors might tell families they will meet their loved ones in heaven as a means of consolation, but contemporary thought does not support that belief as it did in the nineteenth century. There is no longer a strong theological commitment.

"The major exception to this caveat is the teaching of The Church of Jesus Christ of Latter-day Saints, whose members are frequently referred to as the Mormons. The modern perspective on heaven—emphasizing the nearness and similarity of the other world to our own and arguing for the eternal nature of love, family, progress, and work—finds its greatest proponent in Latter-day Saints' (LDS) understanding of the afterlife. While most contemporary Christian groups neglect afterlife beliefs, what happens to people after they die is crucial to LDS teachings and rituals. Heavenly theology is the result not of mere speculation, but of revelation given to past and present church leaders. . . .

" . . . There has been . . . no alteration of the LDS understanding of the afterlife since its articulation by Joseph Smith.

If anything, the Latter-day Saints in the twentieth century have become even bolder in their assertion of the importance of their heavenly theology. . . . In the light of what they perceive as a Christian world which has given up belief in heaven, many Latter-day Saints feel even more of a responsibility to define the meaning of death and eternal life."[1]

Latter-day Saints believe fervently in the continuation of our existence beyond the grave. This work celebrates some of those profound truths that have come to us as a part of the prophesied "restitution of all things" (Acts 3:21). We need not remain ignorant of the purpose of life here or the realities of life hereafter, nor need we turn to the writings of uninspired thinkers or those who live on borrowed light. God has raised up inspired spokesmen in our day—anointed servants we sustain as prophets, seers, and revelators—and it is to them, as well as to the scriptures of the Restoration and the gift of the Holy Ghost, that we turn for instruction, correction, and comforting assurance. In this discussion of life after death, we will follow the order in which these monumental truths were delivered to us in this dispensation.

Although we rejoice in all that God has revealed in our day concerning life, death, the spirit world, resurrection and judgment, and the eternal mansions ahead—much of which we will consider briefly in this work—we acknowledge that there is yet more to come, that he who knows the end from the beginning "will yet reveal many great and important things pertaining to the Kingdom of God" (Articles of Faith 1:9). In the spirit of joy and rejoicing, exploration and anticipation, let us begin the sweet journey into the transcendent truths of salvation associated with life after death.

NOTE

1. Colleen McDannell and Bernhard Lang, *Heaven: A History* (New Haven and London: Yale University Press, 1988), 313, 322.

3

CHAPTER 1

Death and Beyond

D eath is a solemn subject, one that most of us would prefer to avoid. We are uncomfortable with having to face up to our own mortality, and though we are eager for the glories that await us after the resurrection, we are extremely nervous about what it takes to get there. Why do we fear death? Some fear death because of their dread of the unknown, the anxiety associated with going to a place they do not understand. Others fear because they do know enough about what lies ahead, and they fret over a profligate lifestyle and the divine justice that awaits them. Others stew over unfinished earthly business. Even the faithful are hesitant to let go, to surrender themselves to the powers of eternity and release their grip on mortality. Surely a God who has power over all things, including death, would be merciful enough to his children to reveal sufficient truth to prepare and comfort us concerning what lies ahead. And so he has.

Joseph Smith learned very early in his ministry about life beyond the grave. God the Eternal Father and his Son Jesus Christ appeared to the boy prophet in the Sacred Grove in the spring of 1820. The very presence of these two holy personages attested to the reality of the life beyond. Holy

messengers sent to bestow knowledge, keys, and powers testified to the Latter-day Saints that death is not the end. "All
men know they must die," Joseph Smith explained to the
Latter-day Saints in Nauvoo. "And it is important that we
should understand the reasons and causes of our exposure to
the vicissitudes of life and of death, and the designs and purposes of God in our coming into the world, our sufferings
here, and our departure hence. . . . It is but reasonable to suppose that God would reveal something in reference to the
matter, and it is a subject we ought to study more than any
other. We ought to study it day and night, for the world is
ignorant in reference to their true condition and relation. If
we have any claim on our Heavenly Father for anything, it is
for knowledge on this important subject."[1]

THE REALITY OF MORTALITY

There is nothing more common to this life than death; it
is the common lot of all who come into this life to leave it.
Everyone is born, and everyone must die. All are born as helpless infants, and all depart this sphere equally helpless in the
face of death. Even among those who read by the lamp of
gospel understanding, death is frequently viewed with fear
and trembling. Wilford Woodruff "referred to a saying of
Joseph Smith, which he heard him utter (like this), That if the
people knew what was behind the veil, they would try by
every means to . . . get there. But the Lord in his wisdom had
implanted the fear of death in every person that they might
cling to life and thus accomplish the designs of their Creator."[2]

Strictly speaking, there is no death and there are no dead.
When things die, they do not cease to be; they merely cease
to be in this world. Life goes on. Death is a transition, a
change in assignment, a transfer to another realm. When we
die, the spirit continues to see and act and feel and associate;
only the physical body becomes inactive and lifeless for a

season. And so the term *death* describes what we perceive from our limited perspective. From an eternal vantage point, however, there is only life.

We speak often of a person's "untimely death." Generally we mean that it is untimely for us, for those who remain behind. Though it is true that individuals may hasten their death and thus shorten the day of their probation, for the faithful there is nothing untimely about death. We understand so little about life, death, the transition into the next world, and what lies ahead. We cannot look into the hearts or search the minds of individuals in this life, and we do not always know why they do what they do. We dare not judge either the nature of their circumstances here or what the Lord will do to right all wrongs hereafter. President Joseph Fielding Smith stated: "May I say for the consolation of those who mourn, and for the comfort and guidance of all of us, that no righteous man is ever taken before his time. In the case of the faithful saints, they are simply transferred to other fields of labor. The Lord's work goes on in this life, in the world of spirits, and in the kingdoms of glory where men go after their resurrection."[3]

Truly, death passes upon us all to fulfill "the merciful plan of the great Creator" (2 Nephi 9:6). Death is merciful in that it delivers us from the toils and agonies of this life. "When men are prepared," the Prophet Joseph Smith observed, "they are better off to go hence."[4]

Death is merciful, too, because it opens us to a new phase of life, a time wherein the restrictions of this mortal coil are gone and the mind and spirit can soar. President Brigham Young, in speaking of the glory of what lies ahead, remarked: "I can say with regard to parting with our friends, and going ourselves, that I have been near enough to understand eternity so that I have had to exercise a great deal more faith to desire to live than I ever exercised in my whole life to live.

7

The brightness and glory of the next apartment is inexpressible. It is not encumbered with this clog of dirt we are carrying around here so that when we advance in years we have to be stubbing along and to be careful lest we fall down. We see our youth, even, frequently stubbing their toes and falling down. But yonder, how different! They move with ease and like lightning."⁵ "How do we know," asked Elder Orson Pratt, "when this spirit is freed from this mortal tabernacle, but that all [our] senses will be greatly enlarged?

" . . . Unclothe the spirit, and instead of exposing a small portion of it about the size of a pea to the action of the rays of light, the whole of it would be exposed. I think we could then see in different directions at once. . . . I believe we shall be freed, in the next world, in a great measure, from these narrow, contracted methods of thinking. Instead of thinking in one channel, and following up one certain course of reasoning to find a certain truth, knowledge will rush in from all quarters . . . , informing the spirit, and giving understanding concerning ten thousand things at the same time; and the mind will be capable of receiving and retaining all."⁶

Losing family members to death is particularly painful, and those of the household of faith are not spared such feelings. "Thou shalt live together in love, insomuch that thou shalt weep for the loss of them that die" (D&C 42:45). We weep, and we long for a reassociation, but we do not grieve as do those who have no hope (1 Thessalonians 4:13), for to do so is to express a lack of faith in the purposes and plan of God and to ignore the promise of reunion and restoration. To be sure, life's bitter winters may find us walking alone. During those cold and dark seasons of solitude, we wrap ourselves in the protective clothing of faith and its perspective and are warmed by precious memories. Thus we move on, seeking always to view things as God views them. "Precious in the sight of the Lord," the scripture declares, "is the death of his saints" (Psalm 116:15). We have the assurance from modern revelation that "those that die shall rest from all their labors, and their works shall follow them; and they shall receive a crown in the mansions of my Father, which I have prepared for them" (D&C 59:2).

Truly, the Prophet Joseph Smith taught, "this life is not all; the voice of reason, the language of inspiration, and the Spirit of the living God, our Creator, teaches us, as we hold the record of truth in our hands, that this is not the case, that this is not so; for, the heavens declare the glory of a God, and the firmament showeth His handiwork."[7] We are born, and we die. Thus the cycle of life continues everlastingly. If there were no death, there would be no life. If there were no death, then the growth and development and expansion and deification that lie ahead would be forever withheld from us. There is purpose in life, and there is purpose in death. He who knows all things orchestrates the events of our existence and knows what is best for us.

THE WORLD OF SPIRITS

There is never a time when we cease to be. Modern prophets and modern scripture attest that the transition from time into eternity is immediate. As we breathe our last breath, our spirit leaves the body and passes directly into the post-mortal spirit world. Joseph Smith taught: "The spirits of the just are exalted to a greater and more glorious work; hence they are blessed in their departure to the world of spirits. Enveloped in flaming fire, *they are not far from us,* and know and understand our thoughts, feelings, and motions, and are often pained therewith."[8] "Is the spirit world here?" President Brigham Young asked. "It is not beyond the sun, but is on this earth that was organized for the people that have lived and that do and will live upon it."[9] Elder Parley P. Pratt similarly explained that the spirit world "is here on the very planet where we were born."[10]

At the time an individual enters the spirit world, he or she experiences what President Joseph F. Smith called a "partial judgment."[11] The person goes either to paradise or to hell (1 Nephi 15:29; 2 Nephi 9:12). Paradise is the abode of the faithful, a state of happiness, "a state of rest, a state of peace, where they shall rest from all their troubles and from all care, and sorrow" (Alma 40:12). President Joseph F. Smith said further, "Paradise is a place where spirits expand in wisdom, where they have respite from all their troubles, and where care and sorrow do not annoy."[12] On the other hand, the spirits of the wicked "shall be cast out into outer darkness; there shall be weeping, and wailing, and gnashing of teeth, and this because of their own iniquity, being led captive by the devil" (Alma 40:13).

Modern revelation also makes clear that the entire spirit world, not just that portion known as hell or outer darkness, is in a sense a "spirit prison." Though there are divisions of some kind between the righteous and the wicked, all the spirits of men and women are in one world, just as they are in the flesh. In the postmortal spirit world, the disembodied long for deliverance and seek relief from their present condition; they look upon the long absence of their spirits from their bodies as a bondage (D&C 45:17; 138:50; see also 138:15–18, 23). "When our spirits leave these bodies, will they be happy?" Elder Orson Pratt asked. "Not perfectly so," he responded. "Why? Because the spirit is absent from the body; it cannot be perfectly happy while a part of the man is lying in the earth. . . . You will be happy, you will be at ease in paradise; but still you will be looking for a house where your spirit can enter and act as you did in former times."[13]

President Brigham Young asked: "Where are the spirits of the ungodly? They are in prison. Where are the spirits of the righteous, the Prophets, and the Apostles? They are in prison, brethren; that is where they are." He continued: "I know it is a startling idea to say that the Prophet and the persecutor of the Prophet, all go to prison together . . . , but they have not got their bodies yet, consequently they are in prison."[14] The Prophet Joseph Smith summarized: "Hades, the Greek, or Sheol, the Hebrew, these two significations mean a world of spirits. Hades, Sheol, paradise, spirits in prison, are all one: it is a world of spirits."[15] Thus for the apostle Peter to declare that Jesus went after his mortal death to preach to the "spirits in prison" (1 Peter 3:18–20), and knowing from modern scripture that the Master did not minister in person to the wicked (D&C 138:20–22, 29, 37), we conclude that he preached to the spirits in prison in the sense that he preached the gospel in the spirit world. More specifically, "from among the righteous, he organized his forces and appointed messengers, clothed with power and authority, and commissioned them to go forth and carry the light of the gospel to them that were in darkness, even to all the spirits of men" (D&C 138:30).

Just as there are variations among the godly in paradise, so must there also be differences among those in hell. There are the very wicked who, as Alma explained, are subject to confrontation, suffering, and sore repentance. There are others—good people, on the whole—who have not enjoyed the blessings of the fulness of the gospel because such were unavailable to them. These work and grow and learn and develop. Many of them open their hearts to the gospel message and are taught. The Prophet Joseph Smith further clarified that once the gospel message is delivered and accepted by individuals in the spirit world, and once the appropriate ordinances have been performed by those in the flesh who act as proxy for the departed, "the Lord has administrators there to set them free."[16] That is, once a person has received the gospel and its saving ordinances, he or she is permitted to cross the gulf that separates hell from paradise and thereafter enjoy sweet association with the faithful (Luke 16:26; 1 Nephi 15:28–30).[17]

We do not suppose, knowing as we do the goodness and justice of our God, that it would be any easier to accept the gospel as a disembodied spirit than it would to accept it as a mortal (1 Peter 4:6). And yet there are factors that bear upon a person's capacity to see and feel and hear and receive the truth. Some of those factors bear upon all of us, and some of them are beyond our power to control. As we move closer to the great millennial day, wickedness will widen and malevolence will increase. The index of moral pollution will rise, thus making it more and more difficult to remain unscathed and unwounded in the war against evil. Nevertheless, Elder Boyd K. Packer testified, "It is my conviction that those wicked influences one day will be overruled."[18]

"In this space between death and the resurrection of the body, the two classes of souls remain, in happiness or in misery, until the time which is appointed of God that the dead shall come forth and be reunited both spirit and body," declared President Joseph F. Smith.[19] And so the postmortal spirit world is an intermediate stop for all men and women. It is a place of waiting, of repentance and suffering, of peace and rest, and of instruction and preparation. Those who receive and enjoy the blessings of the gospel (celestial), or who at least receive the testimony of Jesus (terrestrial), will come forth from the spirit world unto the first resurrection (D&C 76:50–51, 70–78, 82). Those who continue to assert their own will and refuse the Savior's offer of enlightenment and renewal will remain in the spirit world until the thousand years are ended. Then in that second, or last, resurrection they will come forth either to a telestial glory or to a kingdom of no glory as sons of perdition (D&C 76:32–44; 88:24).

"THIS DAY . . . IN PARADISE"

On Golgotha Jesus hung on the cross between two thieves. One of them "railed on him, saying, If thou be Christ, save thyself and us. But the other answering rebuked him, saying, Dost not thou fear God, seeing thou art in the same condemnation? And we indeed justly; for we receive the due reward of our deeds: but this man hath done nothing amiss. And he said unto Jesus, Lord, remember me when thou comest into thy kingdom. And Jesus said unto him, Verily I say unto thee, To day shalt thou be with me in paradise" (Luke 23:39–43).

As we might expect, this passage has given rise to a whole host of interpretations, perhaps the most prevalent being a belief in deathbed repentance. To be sure, it is good to repent, no matter when we do it. That is, it is better to repent than to remain in our sins. And it is true that the Prophet Joseph Smith taught: "There is never a time when the spirit is too old to approach God. All are within the reach of pardoning mercy, who have not committed the unpardonable sin."[20]

Although we would never denigrate the value of sincere repentance—no matter how late in one's mortal probation (Matthew 20:1–16)—we acknowledge the divine word that "he that repents and does the commandments of the Lord shall be forgiven" (D&C 1:32). The Savior affirmed, "Not every one that saith unto me, Lord, Lord, shall enter into the kingdom of heaven, but he that doeth the will of my Father which is in heaven" (Matthew 7:21). The Prophet Joseph Smith taught that "the infidel will grasp at every straw for help until death stares him in the face, and then his infidelity takes its flight, for the realities of the eternal world are resting upon him in mighty power; and when every earthly support and prop fails him, he then sensibly feels the eternal truths of the immortality of the soul. We should take warning and not wait for the death-bed to repent. . . . Let this, then, prove as a warning to all not to procrastinate repentance, or wait till a death-bed, for it is the will of God that man should repent and serve him in health, and in the strength and power of his mind, in order to secure his blessing, and not wait until he is called to die."[21]

We must look a little deeper into this matter to understand what the Savior really said. Did the Master actually promise the thief on the cross that he would at the time of death enter into paradise, the abode of the righteous? Would all his sins be overlooked? Joseph Smith stated: "I will say something about the spirits in prison. There has been much said by modern divines about the words of Jesus (when on the cross) to the thief, saying, 'This day shalt thou be with me in paradise.' King James' translators make it out to say paradise. But what is paradise? It is a modern word: it does not answer at all to the original word that Jesus made use of [presumably the word *hades*]. Find the original of the word *paradise*. You might as easily find a needle in a haymow. Here is a chance for battle, ye learned men. There is nothing in the original word in Greek from which this was taken that signifies paradise; but it was—'This day thou shalt be with me in the world of spirits.'"[22]

RESURRECTION AND JUDGMENT

If Jesus' greatest accomplishments consisted of his kindness, his generosity, and his sage advice, then our hope for happiness hereafter is unfounded (1 Corinthians 15:19). Like Paul, the Book of Mormon prophet Jacob declared that if Christ did not rise from the dead as it was prophesied that he would do, then we would one and all, at the time of death, be consigned to spiritual ruin and destruction—we would be forevermore subject to the father of lies. Why? Because if Jesus did not have the power to rise from the dead and thus redeem the body from the grave, then he surely does not have the power to forgive sins and thereby redeem the spirit from hell (2 Nephi 9:7–9; 1 Corinthians 15:12–17). "If the resurrection from the dead be not an important point, or item in our faith," the Prophet Joseph Smith explained, "we must confess that we know nothing about it; for if there be no resurrection from the dead, then Christ has not risen; and if Christ has not risen He was not the Son of God." On the other hand, "if He has risen from the dead the bands of the temporal death are broken that the grave has no victory. If then, the grave has no victory, those who keep the sayings of Jesus and obey His teachings have not only a promise of a resurrection from the dead, but an assurance of being admitted into His glorious kingdom."[23] Because Jesus Christ has risen from the dead, we also shall rise from the dead. Because he lives, we also shall live, beyond the grave.

The resurrected body is a spiritual body, meaning that it is immortal, not subject to death (1 Corinthians 15:44; Alma 11:45; D&C 88:27). The scriptural promise is that we come forth from the grave with a resurrected body suited to the kingdom we shall inherit: "They who are of a celestial spirit shall receive the same body which was a natural body; even ye shall receive your bodies, and your glory shall be that glory by which your bodies are quickened. Ye who are quickened by a portion of the celestial glory shall then receive of the same, even a fulness. And they who are quickened by a portion of the terrestrial glory shall then receive of the same, even a fulness. And also they who are quickened by a portion of the telestial glory shall then receive of the same, even a fulness. And they who remain [the sons of perdition] shall also be quickened; nevertheless, they shall return again to their own place, to enjoy that which they are willing to receive, because they were not willing to enjoy that which they might have received" (D&C 88:28–32).

The scriptures of the Restoration also clarify the nature of the resurrected body. "The soul [meaning, the spirit] shall be restored to the body," Alma explained, "and the body to the soul; yea, and every limb and joint shall be restored to its body; yea, even a hair of the head shall not be lost; but all things shall be restored to their proper and perfect frame" (Alma 40:23; see also 11:43). In speaking of the righteous who waited anxiously for the Savior's entrance into paradise, President Joseph F. Smith wrote: "Their sleeping dust was to be restored unto its perfect frame, bone to his bone, and the sinews and the flesh upon them, the spirit and the body to be united never again to be divided, that they might receive a fulness of joy" (D&C 138:17). Latter-day prophets have taught that the body comes forth from the grave as it is laid down, "whether old or young; there will not be 'added unto their stature one cubit,' neither taken from it; all will be raised by the power of God, having spirit in their bodies, and not blood."[24] Yet physical deformities will not be a part of the resurrected body, for "deformity will be removed; defects will be eliminated, and men and women shall attain to the perfection of their spirits, to the perfection that God designed in the beginning."[25]

On one occasion Elder Orson Pratt pointed out that a person's mortal body is constantly changing—old cells being replaced by new ones, and so forth. The Prophet Joseph responded: "There is no fundamental principle belonging to a human system that ever goes into another in this world or in the world to come; I care not what the theories of men are. We have the testimony that God will raise us up, and he has the power to do it. If any one supposes that any part of our bodies, that is, the fundamental parts thereof, ever goes into another body, he is mistaken."[26] President Brigham Young said: "The question may be asked, do not the particles that compose man's body, when returned to mother earth, go to make or compose other bodies? No, they do not. . . . Neither can the particles which have comprised the body of man become parts of the bodies of other men, or of beasts, fowls, fish, insect, or vegetables. They are governed by divine law and though they may pass from the knowledge of the scientific world, that divine law still holds, governs and controls them. Man's body may be buried in the ocean, it may be eaten by wild beasts, or it may be burned to ashes, they may be scattered to the four winds, yet the particles of which it is composed will not be incorporated into any form of vegetable or animal life, to become a component part of their structure. . . . At the sound of the trumpet of God every particle of our physical structures necessary to make our tabernacles perfect will be assembled, to be rejoined with the spirit, every man in his order. Not one particle will be lost."[27]

We have the comforting assurance that even though we will be refined, renewed, and perfected, body and soul, in the resurrection, we will maintain our identity. We will know friends and loved ones in and after the resurrection, even as we know them now. Though Christians at the time of Joseph Smith (and many today, as well) spoke of being caught up into the love of Jesus and blending into his nature, the revelations of heaven declare otherwise. In speaking of meeting a departed loved one in the future, President Joseph F. Smith taught: "I expect to be able to recognize her, just as I could recognize her tomorrow, if she were living . . . , because her identity is fixed and indestructable, just as fixed and indestructable as the identity of God the Father and Jesus Christ the Son. They cannot be any other than themselves. They cannot be changed; they are from everlasting to everlasting, eternally the same; so it will be with us. We will progress and develop and grow in wisdom and understanding, but our identity can never change."[28]

In the Book of Mormon, resurrection and eternal judgment are companion doctrines, just as are the doctrines of the

Fall and the Atonement. One of the great acts of mercy and grace is that all men and women who took a physical body, including the sons of perdition, will be resurrected and thereafter brought to stand before God to be judged of their works. In a sense, therefore, the Atonement overcomes spiritual death for all, at least for a short season in which we stand once again in the divine presence. Jacob wrote: "And it shall come to pass that when all men shall have passed from this first death unto life, insomuch as they have become immortal, they must appear before the judgment-seat of the Holy One of Israel; and then cometh the judgment, and then must they be judged according to the holy judgment of God" (2 Nephi 9:15). Samuel the Lamanite also declared that Jesus "surely must die that salvation may come; yea, it behooveth him and becometh expedient that he dieth, to bring to pass the resurrection of the dead, that thereby men may be brought into the presence of the Lord" (Helaman 14:15; 3 Nephi 27:13–16). Finally, Moroni bore witness that "because of Jesus Christ came the redemption of man. And because of the redemption of man, which came by Jesus Christ, they are brought back into the presence of the Lord; yea, this is wherein all men are redeemed" (Mormon 9:12–13).

Conclusion

"More painful to me are the thoughts of annihilation than death," Joseph Smith once declared.[29] With the restoration of divine truths concerning life after death, light has replaced darkness, sound doctrine and pure religion have replaced ignorance and superstition, and men and women may traverse life's paths without the ominous fear of what, if anything, follows death. We know where we came from. We know why we are here. And we know where we are going when death calls each of us. When we pass through the veil that separates time and eternity, we will know the truth of the testimony with which holy writ resounds: in Christ there is peace. In Christ there is hope, hope for deliverance from sin and death. There are no wrongs that shall not be righted in time or in eternity, no burdens that shall not be lifted. Joseph Smith the Seer, with a perspective informed by a panoramic vision, promised: "All your losses will be made up to you in the resurrection, provided you continue faithful. By the vision of the Almighty I have seen it."[30]

NOTES

1. Joseph Smith, *Teachings of the Prophet Joseph Smith*, sel. Joseph Fielding Smith (Salt Lake City: Deseret Book, 1976), 324.
2. *Diary of Charles L. Walker*, ed. A. Karl Larson and Kathrine Miles Larson, 2 vols. (Logan: Utah State University Press, 1980), 1:595–96; spelling and punctuation standardized.
3. Joseph Fielding Smith, address given at the funeral of Richard L. Evans, 4 November 1971, typescript, 2; see also Spencer W. Kimball, *Faith Precedes the Miracle* (Salt Lake City: Deseret Book, 1984), 103, 105.
4. Smith, *Teachings of the Prophet Joseph Smith*, 326.
5. Brigham Young, *Journal of Discourses*, 26 vols. (London: Latter-day Saints' Book Depot, 1851–86), 14:231.
6. Orson Pratt, *Journal of Discourses*, 2:243, 246.
7. Smith, *Teachings of the Prophet Joseph Smith*, 56.
8. Smith, *Teachings of the Prophet Joseph Smith*, 326.
9. Brigham Young, *Journal of Discourses*, 3:372.
10. Parley P. Pratt, *Key to the Science of Theology* (Salt Lake City: Deseret Book, 1978), 80.
11. Joseph F. Smith, *Gospel Doctrine* (Salt Lake City: Deseret Book, 1971), 448.
12. Smith, *Gospel Doctrine*, 448.
13. Orson Pratt, *Journal of Discourses*, 1:289–90.
14. Brigham Young, *Journal of Discourses*, 3:94–95.
15. Smith, *Teachings of the Prophet Joseph Smith*, 310.
16. Smith, *Teachings of the Prophet Joseph Smith*, 367.
17. Joseph Fielding Smith, *Doctrines of Salvation*, comp. Bruce R. McConkie, 3 vols. (Salt Lake City: Bookcraft, 1954–56), 2:158, 230.
18. Boyd K. Packer, Conference Report, April 1992, 94.
19. Smith, *Gospel Doctrine*, 448.
20. Smith, *Teachings of the Prophet Joseph Smith*, 191.
21. Smith, *Teachings of the Prophet Joseph Smith*, 197.
22. Smith, *Teachings of the Prophet Joseph Smith*, 309.
23. Smith, *Teachings of the Prophet Joseph Smith*, 62.
24. Smith, *Teachings of the Prophet Joseph Smith*, 199–200.
25. Smith, *Gospel Doctrine*, 23.

26. Joseph Smith, *History of the Church of Jesus Christ of Latter-day Saints*, ed. B. H. Roberts, 2d ed. rev., 7 vols. (Salt Lake City: Deseret Book, 1973), 5:339.
27. Brigham Young, "The Resurrection," general conference address, 8 October 1875; in *Elders' Journal* 1 (July 1904): 153.
28. Smith, *Gospel Doctrine*, 25.
29. Smith, *Teachings of the Prophet Joseph Smith*, 296.
30. Smith, *Teachings of the Prophet Joseph Smith*, 296.

More Kingdoms Than One

W hile meeting with his chosen disciples at the Last Supper, the Master said: "Let not your heart be troubled: ye believe in God, believe also in me. In my Father's house are many mansions: if it were not so, I would have told you. I go to prepare a place for you" (John 14:1–2). This is a most intriguing statement. The Savior seems to have been saying, in essence, that it should be obvious, self-evident, to anyone that life hereafter consists of more than merely a heaven and a hell; if it were not so, he would have told us otherwise. Reason suggests that not all people are equally good and thus not all good people deserve the same reward hereafter. Likewise, not all bad people are equally bad and surely some are so bad they deserve to sink to the lowest pit in hell. Something so fundamental, so central to salvation as this principle of justice would surely be a part of what God would make known during the times of restitution.

BACKGROUND

In June 1830 the Prophet Joseph Smith began an inspired translation of the King James Version of the Bible, a labor to which he was divinely directed and appointed, a work he considered to be a "branch of [his] calling."[1] The Prophet and his scribes progressed through the book of Genesis until 7 March 1831, when the Lord commanded the Prophet to turn his attention to the New Testament (D&C 45:60–61). On 12 September 1831, to escape persecution, Joseph Smith relocated to Hiram, Ohio, to live with the John Johnson family.

By 16 February 1832 the Prophet and his scribe, Sidney Rigdon, had translated much of the fifth chapter of John. In verses 28 and 29 the Savior indicates that the time will come when the dead will hear the voice of the Son of God and will come forth from the graves: "They that have done good, unto the resurrection of life; and they that have done evil, unto the resurrection of damnation." The Prophet felt impressed to alter the text as follows: "And shall come forth; they who have done good, in the resurrection of *the just;* and they who have done evil, in the resurrection of *the unjust*" (JST John 5:29; D&C 76:17). "Now this caused us to marvel," the Prophet stated, "for it was given unto us of the Spirit. And while we meditated upon these things, the Lord touched the eyes of our understandings and they were opened, and the glory of the Lord shone round about" (D&C 76:18–19). The alteration in the text, though interesting, is not earthshaking or overwhelming. But truly, "out of small things proceedeth that which is great" (D&C 64:33). There came to Joseph Smith and his scribe on this occasion one of the most remarkable oracles ever given to men on earth, one we have come to know simply as the vision, or the vision of the glories, which is recorded in Doctrine and Covenants 76. This grand revelation stands for Latter-day Saints as an interpretive commentary upon the Savior's words concerning "many mansions" in the world to come.

Philo Dibble, one who was present at the Johnson home when this vision was received, has left us the following fascinating account: "The vision of the three degrees of glory which is recorded in the Doctrine and Covenants was given at the house of 'Father Johnson,' in Hiram, Ohio, and during the time that Joseph and Sidney were in the Spirit and saw the heavens open there were other men in the room, perhaps twelve, among whom I was one during a part of the time—probably two-thirds of the time. I saw the glory and felt the power, but did not see the vision.

"Joseph wore black clothes, but at this time seemed to be dressed in an element of glorious white, and his face shone as if it were transparent, but I did not see the same glory attending Sidney. . . .

"Joseph would, at intervals, say: 'What do I see?' as one might say while looking out the window and beholding what all in the room could not see. Then he would relate what he had seen or what he was looking at.

"Then Sidney replied, 'I see the same.'

"Presently Sidney would say, 'What do I see?' and would repeat what he had seen or was seeing.

"And Joseph would reply, 'I see the same.'

"This manner of conversation was repeated at short intervals to the end of the vision, and during the whole time not a word was spoken by any other person. Not a sound or motion was made by anyone but Joseph and Sidney, and it seemed to me that they never moved a joint or limb during the time I was there, which I think was over an hour, and to the end of the vision.

"Joseph sat firmly and calmly all the time in the midst of a magnificent glory, but Sidney sat limp and pale, apparently as

23

limber as a rag, observing which, Joseph remarked, smilingly, 'Sidney is not used to it as I am.'"²

After the vision and while still in the Spirit, the Prophet and his scribe were permitted to record a hundredth part of what they saw and experienced.³ In fact, the vision actually consists of six visions, each of which we will now consider briefly.

VISION I: THE GLORY OF THE SON

The first vision briefly sets the stage for what follows by placing things in perspective with regard to the work of redemption and salvation—namely, that salvation is in Christ and comes through the shedding of his own blood and his glorious rise to newness of life in the resurrection. The translators thus saw in vision "the glory of the Son, on the right hand of the Father, and received of his fulness; and saw the holy angels, and them who are sanctified before his throne, worshiping God, and the Lamb, who worship him forever and ever" (D&C 76:20–21). Similarly, John the Revelator had recorded concerning the Redeemer, "Ten thousand times ten thousand, and thousands of thousands; saying with a loud voice, Worthy is the Lamb that was slain to receive power, and riches, and wisdom, and strength, and honour, and glory and blessing" (Revelation 5:11–12).

The Prophet and his scribe bore witness of the Redeemer in powerful language: "And now, after the many testimonies which have been given of him, this is the testimony, last of all, which we give of him: That he lives! For we saw him, even on the right hand of God; and we heard the voice bearing record that he is the Only Begotten of the Father—That by him, and through him, and of him, the worlds are and were created, and the inhabitants thereof are begotten sons and daughters unto God" (D&C 76:22–24). Truly, the testimony of Jesus is the spirit of prophecy (Revelation 19:10), and all the holy prophets, from the beginning, have testified of the One who called and sent them (Acts 10:43; Jacob 4:4; 7:11; Mosiah 13:33).

In addition, the Prophet Joseph's witness contains significant doctrine. For one thing, his testimony affirms the burden of scripture—that Jehovah-Christ was and is the Creator of worlds without number (Moses 1:33; 7:30; Ephesians 3:9; Hebrews 1:1–2). It confirms also the infinite and eternal nature of the Atonement. Whatsoever our Lord and Master creates, he redeems. That is to say, his redemptive labors reach beyond the bounds of our earth (Moses 1:32–35).

In 1843 the Prophet Joseph Smith rewrote this vision in poetry. Verses 22 through 24 were rendered as follows:

> And now after all of the proofs made of him,
> By witnesses truly, by whom he was known,
> This is mine, last of all, that he lives; yea he lives!
> And sits at the right hand of God, on his throne.
>
> And I heard a great voice, bearing record from heav'n.
> He's the Savior, and only begotten of God—
> By him, of him, and through him, the worlds were all made,
> Even all that careen in the heavens so broad,
>
> Whose inhabitants, too, from the first to the last,
> Are sav'd by the very same Savior of ours;
> And, of course, are begotten God's daughters and sons,
> By the very same truths, and the very same pow'rs.[4]

Or, as Elder Bruce R. McConkie wrote: "Christ created worlds without number whose inhabitants are adopted into the family of God by the atoning sacrifice wrought on our earth. The faithful on all worlds are spiritually begotten in the same way as on our earth."[5]

VISION II: THE FALL OF LUCIFER

Having been shown that the foundation of our faith is redemption in Christ, the Prophet and Sidney Rigdon learned a vital element of the plan of salvation—the nature of opposition through Satan and satanic influences. Lucifer is described in the vision as one "who was in authority in the presence of God" (D&C 76:25), who rebelled against the Father and the Son in the premortal council in heaven, thus becoming known as *perdition*, a word meaning "ruin" or "destruction." Because he was indeed a spirit son of God, our spirit brother, "a son of the morning" (D&C 76:26), in fact, "one of the early born spirit children of the Father,"[6] the heavens wept over his defection. He coveted the throne of the Father and proposed to save all the sons and daughters of God in a way contrary to the plan of the Father (Moses 4:1–4). "The contention in heaven was—Jesus said there would be certain souls that would not be saved; and the devil said he could save them all, and laid his plans before the grand council, who gave their vote in favor of Jesus Christ. So the devil rose up in rebellion against God, and was cast down, with all who put up their heads for him."[7] Lucifer became thereby an enemy to God and to all righteousness: "Wherefore, he maketh war with the saints of God, and encompasseth them round about" (D&C 76:25–29).

VISION III: THE SONS OF PERDITION

Doctrine and Covenants 76:30–49 describes those who have once known light and truth and the revelations of heaven and who choose knowingly to deny the light and defy God and his work. These are the sons of perdition, "vessels of wrath, doomed to suffer the wrath of God, with the devil and his angels in eternity" (D&C 76:33). The apostle Paul observed that "it is impossible for those who were once enlightened, and have tasted of the heavenly gift, and were made partakers of the Holy Ghost, and have tasted the good word of God, and the powers of the world to come, if they shall fall away, to renew them again unto repentance" (Hebrews 6:4–6; compare 10:26–29).

"What must a man do to commit the unpardonable sin?" Joseph the Seer asked rhetorically in the King Follett Sermon. "He must receive the Holy Ghost, have the heavens opened unto him, and know God, and then sin against Him. After a man has sinned against the Holy Ghost, there is no repentance for him. He has got to say that the sun does not shine while he sees it; he has got to deny Jesus Christ when the heavens have been opened unto him, and to deny the plan of salvation with his eyes open to the truth of it; and from that time he begins to be an enemy." He continued: "When a man begins to be an enemy to this work, he hunts me, he seeks to kill me, and never ceases to thirst for my blood. He gets the spirit of the devil—the same spirit that they had who crucified the Lord of Life—the same spirit that sins against the Holy Ghost. You cannot save such persons; you cannot bring them to repentance; they make open war, like the devil, and awful is the consequence."[8]

All of the sons and daughters of Adam and Eve will come forth from the grave in the resurrection, including sons of perdition (D&C 88:32). The sons of perdition are guilty of the unpardonable sin (Alma 39:6), a sin not covered by the atonement of Christ, a sin for which no amount of personal suffering will right the wrongs done. There is no forgiveness for them, neither here nor hereafter, for "having denied the Holy Spirit after having received it, and having denied the Only Begotten Son of the Father, having crucified him unto themselves and put him to an open shame" (D&C 76:34–35), they are guilty of shedding innocent blood, meaning the innocent blood of Christ.[9] "The blasphemy against the Holy Ghost," a later revelation affirms, "which shall not be forgiven in the world nor out of the world, is in that ye commit murder wherein ye shed innocent blood, and assent unto my death,

27

after ye have received my new and everlasting covenant, saith the Lord God" (D&C 132:27).

The sons of perdition are the only ones who shall be subject to the second spiritual death, the final expulsion from the presence of God. They, after being resurrected and standing before God to be judged (2 Nephi 9:15) shall be consigned to a kingdom of no glory.

In the midst of this gloomy scene the Lord provides one of the most beautiful descriptions of the gospel of Jesus Christ, the "glad tidings" that "he came into the world, even Jesus, to be crucified for the world, and to bear the sins of the world, and to sanctify the world, and to cleanse it from all unrighteousness; that through him all might be saved whom the Father had put into his power and made by him; who glorifies the Father, and saves all the works of his hands, except those sons of perdition who deny the Son after the Father has revealed him" (D&C 76:40–43).

This third vision ended with a sobering reminder that the particulars of the fate of the sons of perdition have not been revealed (D&C 76:45–48). In 1833 the Prophet Joseph Smith explained that "the Lord never authorized [certain individuals] to say that the devil, his angels, or the sons of perdition, should ever be restored; for their state of destiny was not revealed to man, is not revealed, nor ever shall be revealed, save to those who are made partakers thereof: consequently those who teach this doctrine have not received it of the Spirit of the Lord. Truly Brother Oliver declared it to be the doctrine of devils."[10]

VISION IV: THE CELESTIAL GLORY

The scene shifted as the Prophet Joseph Smith and Sidney Rigdon were permitted to study and learn by contrast—from perdition to exaltation. They beheld the glories of the highest, or celestial, kingdom and provided broad descriptions of those who inhabit the same. They beheld the inhabitants of the "resurrection of the just" (D&C 76:50) which is what we call the first resurrection (Mosiah 15:21–25), the resurrection of celestial and terrestrial persons. Celestial persons are those who receive the testimony of Jesus and accept the terms and conditions of the gospel covenant. They are "baptized after the manner of his burial" and receive the gift of the Holy Ghost, thereby becoming "cleansed from all their sins" (D&C 76:51–52). Those who inherit a celestial glory are they who "overcome by faith" (D&C 76:53), who "withstand every temptation of the devil, with their faith on the Lord Jesus Christ" (Alma 37:33). They overcome the world in forsaking worldliness and carnal attractions and give themselves to the Lord and his work. These are "sealed by the Holy Spirit of promise, which the Father sheds forth upon all those who are just and true" (D&C 76:53). The Holy Spirit of Promise is the Holy Ghost, the Holy Spirit promised to the Saints. Because "the Comforter knoweth all things" (D&C 42:17; Moses 6:61), the Holy Ghost is able to search the souls of men and women and to ascertain the degree to which they have truly yielded their hearts unto God, the degree to which they are "just and true" (D&C 76:53). Thus to be sealed by the Holy Spirit of Promise is to have the ratifying approval of the Holy Ghost upon our lives and upon the ordinances and covenants into which we have entered. It is to have passed the tests of mortality, to have qualified for celestial glory hereafter.

> For these overcome, by their faith and their works,
> Being tried in their life-time, as purified gold,
> And seal'd by the spirit of promise, to life,
> By men called of God, as Aaron of old.[11]

Celestial men and women are "the Church of the Firstborn" (D&C 76:54). The Church of the Firstborn is the "inner circle" of faithful Saints who have proven true and faithful to their covenants. As baptism is the gate to membership in the Church of Jesus Christ on earth, so celestial marriage opens the door to membership in the heavenly church.[12] The Church of the Firstborn is the Church beyond the veil, the organized body of Saints who inherit exaltation. It is made up of those who qualify for the blessings of the Firstborn. Jesus is the Firstborn of the Father and as such is entitled to the birthright. As an act of consummate mercy and grace, our blessed Savior makes it possible for us to inherit, receive, and possess the same blessings he receives, as though each of us were the Firstborn. Those who come into the Church and live worthy of the companionship of the Holy Ghost are born again; they become the sons and daughters of Jesus Christ by adoption (Mosiah 5:1–7). If they continue faithful, receive thereafter the covenants and ordinances of the temple, including the endowment and celestial marriage, and are true to those higher covenants, they will eventually become the sons and daughters of God, meaning the Father.[13] They become heirs of God and joint-heirs, or co-inheritors, with Christ to all that the Father has, including eternal life. "Wherefore, as it is written, they are gods, even the sons of God" (D&C 76:58). President Brigham Young therefore stated that "the ordinances of the house of God are expressly for the Church of the Firstborn."[14]

"They are they who are priests and kings, who have received of his fulness, and of his glory" (D&C 76:56). That is, they are kings and queens, priests and priestesses, men and women who through their steadfastness and immovability in keeping their covenants have received what the prophets call the "fulness of the priesthood" (D&C 124:28). The Prophet Joseph explained in 1843 that "those holding the fulness of the Melchizedek Priesthood are kings and priests of the Most High God, holding the keys of power and blessings."[15] These are they who will accompany the Master when he returns in glory, those who, if they have already passed through the veil

30

of death, will come forth from the grave in glorious immortality. The first resurrection, which began at the time of Christ's resurrection, will thus resume. These are they whose names are written in heaven, in the Lamb's book of life (D&C 88:2), "where God and Christ are the judge of all (D&C 76:68).

And then, lest we should conclude that such persons have attained to this highest degree of glory on their own, through their own merits and mortal accomplishments or without divine assistance, the holy word attests: "These are they who are just men made perfect through Jesus the mediator of the new covenant, who wrought out this perfect atonement through the shedding of his own blood" (D&C 76:69). They are made perfect—whole, complete, fully formed, spiritually mature—through their covenant union with the Savior.

VISION V: THE TERRESTRIAL GLORY

The next vision represents a continuation of the first resurrection, or the resurrection of the just. A broad description of terrestrial beings is given: "Behold, these are they who died without law" (D&C 76:72). We know from Joseph Smith's vision of the celestial kingdom that those who did not have the opportunity to receive the gospel fulness, including little children who die before the age of accountability, but who would have done so if that opportunity had been extended to them, are heirs of the celestial kingdom (D&C 137:7–10). Those who "died without law" are the heathen nations (D&C 45:54), as explained in the poetic version:

> Behold, these are they that have died without law;
> The heathen of ages that never had hope.

Elder Melvin J. Ballard described this group as follows: "Now, I wish to say to you that those who died without law, meaning the pagan nations, for lack of faithfulness, for lack of devotion, in the former life, are obtaining all that they are entitled to. I

31

don't mean to say that all of them will be barred from entrance into the highest glory. Anyone of them that repents and complies with the conditions might also obtain celestial glory, but the great bulk of them shall only obtain terrestrial glory."[17]

The Prophet and his scribe witnessed the final state of those who chose to abide by goodness and equity and decency in their second estate but chose also not to receive and incorporate the fulness of that light and power that derive from the receipt of the everlasting gospel. The terrestrial glory is made up of those who in this life did not receive the testimony of Jesus—the testimony that he is the Savior and Redeemer of mankind—but afterward received it; that is, they received that witness in the postmortal spirit world (D&C 76:73–74). The terrestrial world is also inhabited by those who knew in this life that Jesus was the Christ but who were not valiant enough in that witness to receive the fulness of the gospel when it was presented to them. Or, as the Prophet rendered it poetically:

> Not valiant for truth, they obtain'd not the crown,
> But are of that glory that's typ'd by the moon:
> They are they, that come into the presence of Christ,
> But not to the fulness of God, on his throne.[18]

For that matter, those who have received the fulness of the gospel of Jesus Christ—in our day, those who have joined The Church of Jesus Christ of Latter-day Saints—and then do not prove to be valiant in their testimony, are candidates for the terrestrial degree of glory hereafter.[19]

VISION VI: THE TELESTIAL GLORY

Remembering that celestial persons receive the testimony of Jesus and also the gospel covenant and that terrestrial persons receive the testimony of Jesus but not the gospel covenant, we now learn concerning the inhabitants of the telestial world: "These are they who received not the gospel of Christ, neither the testimony of Jesus" (D&C 76:82; see also D&C 76:101). They "deny not the Holy Spirit" (D&C 76:83). That is, their wickedness is not such as to lead to complete perdition; they do not qualify to become sons of perdition, but they "are thrust down to hell" (D&C 76:84); at the time of their mortal death, they enter into that realm of the postmortal sphere we know as hell and are confronted with their sinfulness. These do not come forth from the grave until the "last resurrection," until the end of the Millennium, "until the Lord, even Christ the Lamb, shall have finished his work" (D&C 76:85).

As is the case with the other kingdoms of glory, there are broad classifications of telestial people. These are they "who are of Paul, and of Apollos, and of Cephas. These are they who say they are some of one and some of another—some of Christ and some of John, and some of Moses, and some of Elias, and some of Esaias, and some of Isaiah, and some of Enoch; but received not the gospel, neither the testimony of Jesus, neither the prophets, neither the everlasting covenant" (D&C 76:99–101). Or, as the Prophet wrote in poetry,

> These are they that came out for Apollos and Paul;
> For Cephas and Jesus, in all kinds of hope;
> For Enoch and Moses, and Peter and John;
> For Luther and Calvin, and even the Pope.
>
> For they never received the gospel of Christ,
> Nor the prophetic spirit that came from the Lord;
> Nor the covenant neither, which Jacob once had;
> They went their own way, and they have their reward.[20]

Further, the telestial kingdom is the final abode of liars, sorcerers, adulterers and whoremongers, and, as John the Revelator learned, of murderers (D&C 76:103; Revelation 21:8; 22:15).

33

Finally, the vision adds the sobering detail that the inhabitants of the telestial world, "as innumerable as the stars in the firmament of heaven, or as the sand upon the seashore," shall be "servants of the Most High; but where God and Christ dwell they cannot come, worlds without end" (D&C 76:109, 112). In short, the celestial body is qualitatively different from the terrestrial or the telestial body. Elder Melvin J. Ballard pointed out that "one who gains possession of the lowest degree of the telestial glory may ultimately arise to the highest degree of that glory, but no provision has been made for promotion from one glory to another. . . . [T]hose who come forth in the celestial glory with celestial bodies have a body that is more refined. It is different. The very fibre and texture of the celestial body is more pure and holy than a telestial or terrestrial body, and a celestial body alone can endure celestial glory. . . . When we have a celestial body it will be suited to the celestial conditions and a telestial body could not endure celestial glory. It would be torment and affliction to them. I have not read in the scripture where there will be another resurrection where we can obtain a celestial body for a terrestrial body. What we receive in the resurrection will be ours forever and forever."[21]

President Spencer W. Kimball wrote: "After a person has been assigned to his place in the kingdom, either in the telestial, the terrestrial or the celestial, or to his exaltation, he will never advance from his assigned glory to another glory. That is eternal! That is why we must make our decisions early in life and why it is imperative that such decisions be right."[22]

Although the telestial kingdom is the lowest of the kingdoms of glory, the inhabitants of that glory shall be "heirs of salvation" in a world that "surpasses all understanding" (D&C 76:88–89). Generally speaking, the word *salvation* means in scripture exactly the same thing as *exaltation* or *eternal life* (D&C 6:13; 14:7; Alma 11:40). There are a few times in scripture, however, when *salvation* refers to something less than exalta-tion (see, for example, D&C 132:17), and this is one of those times. In this expansive sense, our Lord seeks to save all of his children with an everlasting salvation. And he does so, in that all but the sons of perdition eventually inherit a kingdom of glory (D&C 76:43). In fact, Elder Charles W. Penrose observed about the telestial kingdom: "While there is one soul of this race, willing and able to accept and obey the laws of redemp-tion, no matter where or in what condition it may be found, Christ's work will be incomplete until that being is brought up from death and hell, and placed in a position of progress, upward and onward, in such glory as is possible for its enjoy-ment and the service of the great God.

"The punishment inflicted will be adequate to the wrongs performed. In one sense the sinner will always suffer its effects. When the debt is paid and justice is satisfied; when obedience is learned through the lessons of sad experience; when the grateful and subdued soul comes forth from the everlasting punishment, thoroughly willing to comply with the laws once rejected; there will be an abiding sense of loss. The fullness of celestial glory in the presence and society of God and the Lamb are beyond the reach of that saved but not perfected soul, forever. The power of increase, wherein are dominion and exaltation and crowns of immeasurable glory, is not for the class of beings who have been thrust down to hell and endured the wrath of God for the period allotted by eternal judgment. . . .

"Those who were cast down to the depths of their sins, who rejected the gospel of Jesus, who persecuted the Saints, who reveled in iniquity, who committed all manner of trans-gressions except the unpardonable crime, will also come forth in the Lord's time, through the blood of the Lamb and the ministry of His disciples and their own repentance and willing acceptance of divine law, and enter into the various degrees of glory and power and progress and light, according to their different capacities and adaptabilities. They cannot go up into the society of the Father nor receive of the presence of the Son, but will have ministrations of messengers from the terrestrial world, and have joy beyond all expectations and the conception of uninspired mortal minds. They will all bow the knee to Christ and serve God the Father, and have an eternity of usefulness and happiness in harmony with the higher powers. They receive the telestial glory."[23]

The vision is a remarkable oracle. "Nothing could be more pleasing to the Saints upon the order of the Kingdom of the Lord," Joseph Smith stated, "than the light which burst upon the world through the foregoing vision. Every law, every commandment, every promise, every truth, and every point touching the destiny of man, from Genesis to Revelation, . . . witness the fact that the document is a transcript from the records of the eternal world. The sublimity of the ideas; the purity of the language; the scope for action; the continued duration for completion, in order that the heirs of salvation may confess the Lord and bow the knee; the rewards for faithfulness, and the punishments for sins, are so much beyond the narrow-mindedness of men, that every man is constrained to exclaim: 'It came from God.'"[24]

CONCLUSION

The Prophet Joseph Smith and Sidney Rigdon received the vision of the glories in 1832. God continued to reveal himself, his plan, and the doctrines of salvation during the next twelve years of the Prophet Joseph's mortal ministry and subsequently to his successors. Some time after the coming of Elijah and the restoration of the fulness of the priesthood in April 1836, the Prophet Joseph Smith introduced the Saints to the doctrine and practice of celestial marriage. He taught that "in the celestial glory there are three heavens or degrees; and in order to obtain the highest, a man must enter into this order of the priesthood [meaning the new and everlasting covenant of marriage]; and if he does not, he cannot obtain it. He may enter into the other, but that is the end of his kingdom; he cannot have an increase" (D&C 131:1–4). Or, as the Prophet stated another way, "except a man and his wife enter into an everlasting covenant and be married for eternity, while in this probation, by the power and authority of the Holy Priesthood, they will cease to increase when they die; that is, they will not have any children after the resurrection. But those who are married by the power and authority of the priesthood in this life, and continue without committing the sin against the Holy Ghost, will continue to increase and have children in the celestial glory."[25]

Truly there are many mansions of the Father (John 14:1–2), and the Holy One of Israel has made provision for his people to attain to that level of glory hereafter that they are willing to receive. The Prophet quoted the Savior about many mansions and said: "It should be—'In my Father's kingdom are many kingdoms, in order that ye may be heirs of God and joint-heirs with me.' I do not believe the Methodist doctrine of sending honest men and noble-minded men to hell, along with the murderer and the adulterer. They may hurl all their hell and fiery billows upon me, for they will roll off me as fast as they come on. But I have an order of things to save the poor fellows at any rate, and get them saved; for I will send men to preach to them in prison and save them if I can."[26] Here is a message of hope, a breath of fresh air amid the fiery winds of sectarian theology, a doctrine that manifests the mercy and wisdom of our Divine Redeemer. Thanks be to God for the revelations of the Restoration.

NOTES
1. Joseph Smith, *History of The Church of Jesus Christ of Latter-day Saints*, ed. B. H. Roberts, 2d ed. rev., 7 vols. (Salt Lake City: Deseret Book, 1957), 1:238.

2. Cited in *They Knew the Prophet,* comp. Hyrum L. Andrus and Helen Mae Andrus (Salt Lake City: Deseret Book, 1999), 67–68.

3. Joseph Smith, *Teachings of the Prophet Joseph Smith,* sel. Joseph Fielding Smith (Salt Lake City: Deseret Book, 1976), 305; compare D&C 76:115–16.

4. Joseph Smith, *Times and Seasons* 4 (1 February 1843): 82–83, stanzas 18–20.

5. Bruce R. McConkie, *A New Witness for the Articles of Faith* (Salt Lake City: Deseret Book, 1985), 131; see also *Mormon Doctrine,* 2d ed. (Salt Lake City: Bookcraft, 1966), 65.

6. See McConkie, *Mormon Doctrine,* 744.

7. Smith, *Teachings of the Prophet Joseph Smith,* 357.

8. Smith, *Teachings of the Prophet Joseph Smith,* 358.

9. Bruce R. McConkie, *Doctrinal New Testament Commentary,* 3 vols. (Salt Lake City: Bookcraft, 1965–73), 3:345; *New Witness for the Articles of Faith,* 233.

10. Smith, *Teachings of the Prophet Joseph Smith,* 24.

11. Smith, *Times and Seasons* 4 (1 February 1843): 84, stanza 43.

12. See Joseph Fielding Smith, *Doctrines of Salvation,* comp. Bruce R. McConkie, 3 vols. (Salt Lake City: Bookcraft, 1954–56), 2:42; *Man: His Origin and Destiny* (Salt Lake City: Deseret Book, 1954), 272; *The Way to Perfection* (Salt Lake City: Deseret Book, 1970), 208; Bruce R. McConkie, *The Promised Messiah* (Salt Lake City: Deseret Book, 1978), 47; *New Witness for the Articles of Faith,* 337.

13. McConkie, *Doctrinal New Testament Commentary,* 2:472, 475, 491.

14. Brigham Young, *Journal of Discourses,* 26 vols. (London: Latter-day Saints' Book Depot, 1851–86), 8:154.

15. Smith, *Teachings of the Prophet Joseph Smith,* 322.

16. Smith, *Times and Seasons* 4 (1 February 1843): 84, stanza 54.

17. Melvin J. Ballard, "The Three Degrees of Glory," in *Melvin J. Ballard, Crusader for Righteousness* (Salt Lake City: Bookcraft, 1966), 221.

18. Smith, *Times and Seasons* 4 (1 February 1843): 84, stanza 57.

19. Bruce R. McConkie, Conference Report, October 1974, 43–47.

20. Smith, *Times and Seasons* 4 (1 February 1843): 85, stanzas 70–71.

21. Ballard, "Three Degrees of Glory," in *Melvin J. Ballard,* 224–25; see also Smith, *Doctrines of Salvation,* 2:31–34.

22. Spencer W. Kimball, *The Miracle of Forgiveness* (Salt Lake City: Bookcraft, 1969), 243–44.

23. Charles W. Penrose, *"Mormon" Doctrine* (Salt Lake City: George Q. Cannon & Sons, 1897), 72, 74, 75.

24. Smith, *Teachings of the Prophet Joseph Smith,* 11.

25. Smith, *Teachings of the Prophet Joseph Smith,* 300–301.

26. Smith, *Teachings of the Prophet Joseph Smith,* 366; see also 331.

CHAPTER 3

What of Those Who Never Heard?

O ne Evangelical Christian writer asked: "What is the fate of those who die never hearing of the gospel of Christ? Are all the 'heathen' lost? Is there an opportunity for those who have never heard of Jesus to be saved?

"These questions raise one of the most perplexing, provocative and perennial issues facing Christians. It has been considered by philosophers and farmers, Christians and non-Christians. In societies where Christianity has had strong influence, just about everyone has either asked or been asked about the final destiny of those dying without knowledge of the only Savior, Jesus Christ. Far and away, . . . this is the most-asked apologetic question on U.S. college campuses. . . .

"Although there is no way of knowing exactly how many people died without ever hearing about Israel or the church, it seems safe to conclude that the vast majority of human beings who have ever lived fall into this category.

"In terms of sheer numbers, then, an inquiry into the salvation of the unevangelized is of immense interest. What may be said about the destiny of countless billions who have lived and died apart from any understanding of the divine grace manifested in Jesus?"[1]

This issue has been termed "the soteriological problem of evil." *Soteriology* is the study of salvation, and thus the soteriological problem of evil might be stated simply as follows: If in fact Christ is the only name by which salvation comes (Acts 4:12; Mosiah 3:17), and if, as we have seen, most of the human race will go to the grave without ever having heard of Christ in this life, how could God be considered in any way to be a just or merciful Deity?

This is an ancient issue. As early as the fourth century, St. Augustine attempted to respond to Porphyry, a philosopher who opposed Christianity. Porphyry asked: "If Christ declares Himself to be the Way of Salvation, the Grace and the Truth, and affirms that in Him alone, and only to souls believing in Him, is the way of return to God, what has become of men who lived in the many centuries before Christ came? . . . What, then, has become of such an innumerable multitude of souls, who were in no wise blameworthy, seeing that He in whom alone saving faith can be exercised had not yet favored men with His advent?"[2]

As we would suppose, efforts to respond to what is indeed a significant challenge to the Christian faith have been numerous. Some people readily adopt an agnostic position, saying we simply do not know what God intends to do with the unevangelized. Others, who attempt to address the problem, fall into four main categories: (1) exclusivism, or restrictivism; (2) pluralism, or universalism; (3) inclusivism, and (4) postmortem evangelism, or divine perseverance.

Exclusivism, or restrictivism, might be stated thus: People are saved only if they accept the Lord Jesus Christ here and now, in this life. That includes a worship of the only true God, a union with Christ through full acceptance of his saving grace

40

and atonement, and a Christian walk that reflects one's membership in the body of Christ. All others will be damned. There is no chance for salvation or receipt of the gospel hereafter. Those who are Calvinistic, who believe in the election and predestination of souls, would conclude that all who do not receive Christ here were not elected, in God's infinite wisdom and mercy, to do so. Besides, they might add, no one deserves to be saved; we ought to feel intense gratitude for those whom God foreknew and foreappointed to salvation. In short, in this view "our destinies are sealed at death and no opportunity for salvation exists after that."[3]

Pluralism, or universalism, responds to the soteriological problem of evil quite simply: There is goodness and morality in religions and religious practices throughout the world; Christians do not have a monopoly on morality and decency. The philosopher John Hick wrote that the people of the other world religions are on the same moral and spiritual level as Christians. "They seem on average to be neither better nor worse than are Christians." He further observed that "if we define salvation as being forgiven and accepted by God because of Jesus' death on the cross, then it becomes a tautology that Christianity alone knows and is able to preach the source of salvation. But if we define salvation as an actual human change, a gradual transformation from natural self-centeredness (with all the human evils that flow from this) to a radically new orientation centered in God and manifested in the 'fruit of the Spirit,' then it seems clear that salvation is taking place within all of the world religions—and taking place, so far as we can tell, to more or less the same extent." Hick thus argues "on Christian grounds for a doctrine of universal salvation."[4]

Inclusivism is a third approach to this difficult question. Justin Martyr, the early Christian apologist (ca. A.D. 100–165), explained that Christ "is the Word of whom every race of men were partakers; and those who lived reasonably are Christians, even though they have been thought atheists; as among the Greeks, Socrates and Heraclitus, and men like them."[5] Justin Martyr believed that all are partakers of a general revelation through the universal logos, though in Jesus Christ the logos was revealed in its fulness. Likewise, Irenaeus (ca. A.D. 130– 200) contended that God has never been completely unknown to any race of people, inasmuch as the universal Spirit of Christ is inherent in the minds of men and women of all times and places. "For it was not merely for those who believed on Him in the time of Tiberius Caesar that Christ came, nor did the Father exercise his providence for the men only who are now alive, but for all men altogether, who from the beginning, according to their capacity, in their generation have both feared and loved God, and practiced justice and piety towards their neighbors, and have earnestly desired to see Christ, and to hear His voice. Wherefore He shall, at His second coming . . . give them a place in His kingdom."[6]

In the twentieth century, C. S. Lewis wrestled with this question. As an inclusivist, he believed that "those who put themselves in [God's] hands will become perfect, as He is perfect—perfect in love, wisdom, joy, beauty, and immortality. The change will not be completed in this life, for death is an important part of the treatment."[7]

Further, Lewis taught, "Christ saves many who do not think they know Him. For He is (dimly) present in the good side of the inferior teachers they follow. In the Parable of the Sheep and the Goats (Matthew 25), those who are saved do not seem to know that they have served Christ."[8] Lewis also said: "There are people (a great many of them) who are slowly ceasing to be Christians but who still call themselves by that name: some of them are clergymen. There are other people who are slowly becoming Christians though they do not yet call themselves so. There are people who do not accept the full

Christian doctrine about Christ but who are so strongly attracted by Him that they are His in a much deeper sense than they themselves understand. There are people in other religions who are being led by God's secret influence to concentrate on those parts of their religion which are in agreement with Christianity, and who thus belong to Christ without knowing it. . . . Many of the good Pagans long before Christ's birth may have been in this position."[9]

Lewis repeatedly taught that Jesus is the only way to salvation. But although "all salvation is through Christ, we need not conclude that He cannot save those who have not explicitly accepted Him in this life. And it should (at least in my judgment) be made clear that we are not pronouncing all other religions to be totally false, but rather saying that in Christ whatever is true in all religions is consummated and perfected."[10]

In short, while the inclusivist acknowledges that salvation is in Christ alone, he also notes that God is working through his Spirit to bring people to higher light, to that higher light we know as the gospel of Jesus Christ. From this perspective, "God saves people only because of the work of Christ, but people may be saved even if they do not know about Christ. God grants them salvation if they exercise faith in God as revealed to them through creation and providence." Further, "according to the inclusivist view, the Father reaches out to the unevangelized through both the Son and the Spirit via general revelation, conscience and human culture. God does not leave himself without witness to any people. Salvation for the unevangelized is made possible only by the redemptive work of Jesus, but God applies that work even to those who are ignorant of the atonement. God does this if people respond in trusting faith to the revelation they have."[11]

Favorite passages of scripture for inclusivists are Titus 2:11 ("For the grace of God that bringeth salvation hath appeared to all men") and 1 Timothy 2:3–4 ("For this is good and acceptable in the sight of God our Saviour; who will have all men to be saved, and to come unto the knowledge of the truth"). Scriptural illustrations of those who obviously exercised faith but were outside the purview of a traditional Christian reception of the gospel include people mentioned in Hebrews 11, such as Abel, Enoch, Noah, Job, Melchizedek, Jethro (those called "holy pagans"), as well as such premessianic Jews as Abraham and such faithful Gentiles as Cornelius.[12]

Postmortem evangelism, a fourth position taken by some Christians in regard to the soteriological problem of evil, has also been called future probation, second probation, eschatological evangelism, and divine perseverance. According to this view, those who die without a knowledge of the gospel are not damned; they have an opportunity to receive the truth in the world to come. One advocate of this position, Gabriel Fackre, pointed out: "God is resolute, never giving up on getting the Word out. In this world God will give us the power to spread the gospel far and wide. But the Word will also be declared to those we can't reach, even if it takes an eternity." He adds that "God's love is patient and persistent. It outlasts us. . . . For the final victory of this powerful patience, however, we must await the end of the story. Only then will the kingdom come—the resurrection of the dead, the return of Christ, final judgment and everlasting life. In the end, God will settle accounts, vindicate the sufferer and validate the divine purposes."[13]

Respected evangelical Donald Bloesch explained: "We do not wish to build fences around God's grace, . . . and we do not preclude the possibility that some in hell might finally be translated into heaven. The gates of the holy city are depicted as being open day and night (Isa. 60:11; Rev. 21:25), and this means that access to the throne of grace is possible continuously. The gates of hell are locked, but they are locked only from within. C. S. Lewis has suggested in *The Great Divorce* that where there is a supposed transition from hell to

44

heaven the person was never really in hell but only in purgatory. This, of course, is interesting speculation, and may be close to the truth. Yet we must maintain a reverent agnosticism concerning the workings of God's grace which are not revealed in Holy Scripture. We can affirm salvation on the other side of the grave, since this has scriptural warrant."[14]

Favorite passages of scripture for those who espouse the view of postmortem evangelism include 1 Peter 3:18–20 and 1 Peter 4:6, which refer to Christ's teaching the gospel in the postmortal world; John 5:25, in which Jesus states that the dead will hear the voice of the Son of God; and Ephesians 4:8–9, which speaks of Christ descending to the "lower parts of the earth."

CONCLUSION

Truly, those who search the holy scriptures, who encounter the consummate mercy of an all-loving God, cannot help but ask, What of those who never heard, those who through no fault of their own lived and died ignorant of the true way of salvation? One critic of postmortem evangelism, or divine perseverance, stressed that the postmortem evangelism "reading of 1 Peter 4:6 is neither the only nor even the most plausible interpretation. Wise Christians do not base any important doctrine—especially one that is controversial and that might also contain heretical implications—on one single, highly debatable passage of Scripture. If this approach were applied by [postmortem evangelism] advocates to 1 Corinthians 15:29, it would lead Christians to follow a policy of baptizing living people as proxies for the unbaptized dead."[15]

Indeed, it would.

NOTES

1. John Sanders, *What about Those Who Have Never Heard?* (Downers Grove, Ill.: InterVarsity Press, 1995), 7–8, 9; see also Clark Pinnock and Delwin Brown, *Theological Crossfire* (Grand Rapids, Mich.: Zondervan, 1990), 227.

2. In *A Select Library of the Nicene and Post-Nicene Fathers of the Christian Church,* ed. Philip Schaff, Series 1, 14 vols. (Grand Rapids, Mich.: Eerdmans, 1988),1:416.

3. Sanders, *What about Those Who Have Never Heard?* 13.

4. John Hick, in *Four Views on Salvation in a Pluralistic World,* ed. Dennis L. Okholm and Timothy R. Phillips (Grand Rapids, Mich.: Zondervan, 1996), 39, 43, 45.

5. In *The Ante-Nicene Fathers,* ed. Alexander Roberts and James Donaldson, 10 vols. (Grand Rapids, Mich.: Eerdmans, [1956]), 1:178.

6. In Roberts and Donaldson, *Ante-Nicene Fathers,* 1:494.

7. C. S. Lewis, *Mere Christianity* (New York: Touchstone, 1996), 147.

8. C. S. Lewis to Mrs. Ashton, 8 November 1952, in *Letters of C. S. Lewis,* ed. W. H. Lewis, revised by Walter Hooper (New York: Harcourt Brace & Co., 1993), 428.

9. Lewis, *Mere Christianity,* 178.

10. C. S. Lewis, *God in the Dock,* ed. Walter Hooper (Grand Rapids, Mich.: Eerdmans, 1970), 102.

11. In Sanders, *What about Those Who Have Never Heard?* 36–42; *No Other Name* (Grand Rapids, Mich.: Eerdmans, 1992), 259–60; see also Clark Pinnock, *Flame of Love* (Downers Grove, Ill.: InterVarsity Press, 1996), 185–214.

12. Sanders, *What about Those Who Have Never Heard?* 13, 36.

13. Gabriel Fackre, in Sanders, *What about Those Who Have Never Heard?* 73, 78.

14. *Essentials of Evangelical Theology,* 2 vols. (San Francisco: Harper, 1978), 2:226–27.

15. Ronald H. Nash, in Sanders, *What about Those Who Have Never Heard?* 130.

CHAPTER 4

Heirs of the Celestial Kingdom

T he headquarters of the restored Church moved from New York and Pennsylvania to Ohio. By 1831 two Church centers were organized, one in Kirtland and the other in Missouri (Zion). In 1833 the Lord reminded the Saints in Kirtland of his commandment to "build a house, in the which house I design to endow those whom I have chosen with power from on high" (D&C 95:8). After it was built, the Lord rewarded their sacrifices with a marvelous outpouring of light and truth.

A BLESSING MEETING

One Latter-day Saint historian wrote concerning this eventful epoch in our history: "During a fifteen-week period, extending from January 21 to May 1, 1836, probably more Latter-day Saints beheld visions and witnessed other unusual spiritual manifestations than during any other era in the history of the Church. There were reports of Saints' beholding heavenly beings at ten different meetings held during that time. At eight of these meetings, many reported seeing angels; and at five of the services, individuals testified that Jesus, the Savior, appeared. While the Saints were thus communing with heavenly hosts, many prophesied, some spoke in tongues, and others received the gift of interpretation of tongues."[1]

Joseph Smith and other early leaders of the Church had begun to meet in the temple before its completion and had participated in washings, anointings, and blessings, all in preparation for what came to be known as the Kirtland Endowment. On Thursday evening, 21 January 1836, the Prophet and a number of Church leaders from Kirtland and Missouri gathered on the third or attic floor of the Kirtland Temple in the translating room or "President's Room." The Prophet recorded:

"At early candle-light I met with the Presidency at the west school room, in the Temple, to attend to the ordinance of anointing our heads with holy oil; also the [High] Councils of Kirtland and Zion met in the two adjoining rooms, and waited in prayer while we attended to the ordinance. I took the oil in my left hand, Father Smith being seated before me, and the remainder of the Presidency encircled him round about. We then stretched our right hands towards heaven, and blessed the oil, and consecrated it in the name of Jesus Christ.

"We then laid our hands upon our aged Father Smith, and invoked the blessings of heaven. I then anointed his head with the consecrated oil, and sealed many blessings upon him. The Presidency then in turn laid their hands upon his head, . . . and pronounced such blessings upon his head, as the Lord put into their hearts, all blessing him to be our Patriarch, to anoint our heads, and attend to all duties that pertain to that office. The Presidency then . . . received their anointing and blessing under the hands of Father Smith. And in turn, my father anointed my head, and sealed upon me the blessings of

Moses, to lead Israel in the latter days, even as Moses led him in days of old; also the blessings of Abraham, Isaac, and Jacob. All of the Presidency laid their hands upon me, and pronounced upon my head many prophecies and blessings, many of which I shall not notice at this time. But as Paul said, so say I, let us come to visions and revelations."[2]

THE VISION COMMENCES

Joseph the Prophet had learned by vision in February 1832 the nature of those who would inherit the highest heaven, or the celestial kingdom. These persons are they who "overcome by faith, and are sealed by the Holy Spirit of Promise," they "into whose hands the Father has given all things" (D&C 76:53, 55). In the vision given to Joseph Smith in the Kirtland Temple, "the heavens were opened upon us, and I beheld the celestial kingdom of God, and the glory thereof, whether in the body or out I cannot tell. I saw the transcendent beauty of the gate through which the heirs of that kingdom will enter, which was like unto circling flames of fire; also the blazing throne of God, whereon was seated the Father and the Son. I saw the beautiful streets of that kingdom, which had the appearance of being paved with gold" (D&C 137:1–4).

The Prophet was often faced with the challenge of describing glorious events and visions and scenes and revelations with a limited mortal vocabulary. In speaking of the First Vision, for example, he wrote of a pillar of light "above the brightness of the sun" and the Father and the Son as two personages "whose brightness and glory defy all description" (Joseph Smith–History 1:16–17). God thus showed himself to be "a Man of Holiness" (Moses 6:57) with a body of flesh and bones as tangible as our own (D&C 130:22). And he also showed forth his divine nature, a nature that is characterized by such words as light, power, life, spirit, and glory.

The faithful have been promised from the beginning that they may qualify to "dwell with the devouring fire" and dwell with "everlasting burnings" (Isaiah 33:14), that is, dwell with God. "How consoling to the mourners," the Prophet Joseph stated at the funeral service for Elder King Follett, "when they are called to part with a husband, wife, father, mother, child, or dear relative, to know that, although the earthly tabernacle is laid down and dissolved, they shall rise again to dwell in everlasting burnings in immortal glory."[3] "God Almighty Himself dwells in eternal fire," the Prophet said. "Flesh and blood cannot go there, for all corruption is devoured by the fire. 'Our God is a consuming fire.'"[4]

Joseph Smith's vision of the celestial kingdom was not unlike John the Revelator's vision of the holy city, the earth in its sanctified and celestial state: "The foundations of the wall of the city," wrote John, "were garnished with all manner of precious stones." Further, "the street of the city was pure gold, as it were transparent glass" (Revelation 21:19, 21).

ALVIN SMITH: THE SCRIPTURAL PROTOTYPE

Joseph's account of the vision continues: "I saw Father Adam and Abraham; and my father and my mother; my brother Alvin, that has long since slept; and marveled how it was that he had obtained an inheritance in that kingdom, seeing that he had departed this life before the Lord had set his hand to gather Israel the second time, and had not been baptized for the remission of sins" (D&C 137:5–6).

Joseph's vision was a glimpse into the future celestial realm, for he saw his parents in the kingdom of the just, when in fact both were still living in mortality in 1836. Joseph Sr. would not die until 1840 and Mother Smith would live for another twenty years. Father Smith was, interestingly, in the same room with his son at the time the vision was received.

50

The Prophet also saw his brother Alvin, who was the first-born of Joseph Sr. and Lucy Mack Smith. He was born on 11 February 1798 in Tunbridge, Vermont. His was a pleasant and loving disposition, and he constantly sought opportunities to aid the family in their financial struggles. The Prophet described his oldest brother as one in whom there was no guile[5] and as "a very handsome man, surpassed by none but Adam and Seth."[6]

Lucy Mack wrote that on the morning of 15 November 1823, "Alvin was taken very sick with the bilious colic," probably appendicitis. A physician hurried to the Smith home and administered calomel, an experimental drug, to Alvin. The dose of calomel "lodged in his stomach," and on the third day of sickness Alvin became aware that he was going to die. He asked that each of the Smith children come to his bedside for his parting counsel and final expression of love. According to Mother Smith's record, "When he came to Joseph, he said, 'I am now going to die, the distress which I suffer, and the feelings that I have, tell me my time is very short. I want you to be a good boy, and do everything that lies in your power to obtain the Record. [Joseph had been visited by Moroni less than three months before this time.] Be faithful in receiving instruction, and in keeping every commandment that is given you.'"[7]

Alvin died on 19 November 1823. Mother Smith wrote of the pall of grief surrounding his passing: "Alvin was a youth of singular goodness of disposition—kind and amiable, so that lamentation and mourning filled the whole neighborhood in which he resided."[8] Joseph wrote many years later: "I remember well the pangs of sorrow that swelled my youthful bosom and almost burst my tender heart when he died. He was the oldest and noblest of my father's family. . . . He lived without spot from the time he was a child. . . . He was one of the soberest of men, and when he died the angel of the Lord visited him in his last moments."[9]

Because Alvin had died seven years before the organization of the Church and had not been baptized by proper authority, Joseph wondered during his vision how it was possible for his brother to have attained the highest heaven. Alvin's family had been shocked and saddened at his funeral when they heard the Presbyterian minister announce that Alvin would be consigned to hell, having never officially been baptized or involved in the church. William Smith, Alvin's younger brother, recalled: "Hyrum, Samuel, Katherine, and mother were members of the Presbyterian Church. My father would not join. He did not like it because Rev. Stockton had preached my brother's funeral sermon and intimated very strongly that he had gone to hell, for Alvin was not a church member, but he was a good boy and my father did not like it."[10] What joy and excitement must have filled the souls of both Joseph Smith Junior and Senior when they heard the voice of an omniscient and omniloving God saying: "All who have died without a knowledge of this gospel, who would have received it if they had been permitted to tarry, shall be heirs of the celestial kingdom of God; also all that shall die henceforth without a knowledge of it, who would have received it with all their hearts, shall be heirs of that kingdom; for I, the Lord, will judge all men according to their works, according to the desire of their hearts" (D&C 137:7–9).

God does not hold anyone accountable for a gospel law of which he or she was ignorant. Joseph the Prophet learned that every person will have an opportunity—here or hereafter—to accept and apply the principles of the gospel of Jesus Christ. Only the Lord, the Holy One of Israel, is capable of perfect judgment, and thus only he can discern completely the hearts and minds of mortal men. He alone knows when a person has received sufficient knowledge or impressions of the

Spirit to constitute a valid opportunity to receive the message of salvation. This vision reaffirmed that the Lord will judge men not only by their actions but also by their attitudes—the desires of their heart (Alma 41:3).

THE SALVATION OF CHILDREN

Another of the profoundly beautiful doctrines enunciated in the vision of the celestial kingdom deals with the status of children who die. "And I also beheld that all children who die before they arrive at the years of accountability are saved in the celestial kingdom of heaven" (D&C 137:10). This part of the vision affirmed what earlier prophets had taught. King Benjamin had learned from an angel that "the infant perisheth not that dieth in his infancy" (Mosiah 3:18). And after having described the nature of those who will come forth in the first resurrection, Abinadi said simply: "Little children also have eternal life" (Mosiah 15:25). A revelation given to Joseph Smith in September 1830 had specified that "little children are redeemed from the foundation of the world through mine Only Begotten" (D&C 29:46; JST Matthew 19:13–15). And Joseph Smith later taught that "the Lord takes many away, even in infancy, that they may escape the envy of man, and the sorrows and evils of this present world; they were too pure, too lovely, to live on earth; therefore, if rightly considered, instead of mourning we have reason to rejoice as they are delivered from evil, and we shall soon have them again."[11] By virtue of his infinite understanding of the human family, "we may assume that the Lord knows and arranges beforehand who shall be taken in infancy and who shall remain on earth to undergo whatever tests are needed in their cases."[12]

In speaking of the status of children who die before maturity, the Prophet stated: "As concerning the resurrection, I will merely say that all men will come from the grave as they lie down, whether old or young; there will not be 'added unto their stature one cubit,' neither taken from it; all will be raised by the power of God, having spirit in their bodies, and not blood. Children will be enthroned in the presence of God and the Lamb with bodies of the same stature that they had on earth, having been redeemed by the blood of the Lamb; they will there enjoy the fulness of that light, glory and intelligence, which is prepared in the celestial kingdom."[13] Joseph F. Smith, son of Hyrum Smith and the sixth president of the Church, explained: "Joseph Smith declared that the mother who laid down her little child, being deprived of the privilege, the joy, and the satisfaction of bringing it up to manhood or womanhood in this world, would, after the resurrection, have all the joy, satisfaction and pleasure, and even more than it would have been possible to have had in mortality, in seeing her child grow to the full measure of the stature of its spirit."[14]

Will children who die before the age of accountability be subject to temptation and testing? Amulek informed us that our disposition here will be our disposition hereafter (Alma 34:32–35). Such is the case with little children. They were pure in this mortal existence, will be pure in the world of spirits, and will come forth in the resurrection of the pure in heart at the appropriate time. At the time of the second coming of Christ, wickedness will be cleansed from the face of the earth. The Millennium will be ushered in with great power, and then Satan and his hosts will be bound by the righteousness of the people (1 Nephi 22:26). During this glorious time, the earth will be given to the righteous "for an inheritance; and they shall multiply and wax strong, and their children shall grow up without sin unto salvation" (D&C 45:58).

But the devil will be loosed at the end of the Millennium. Could not those who had left mortality without trial be tested during that "little season"? No, for these children will already have come forth from the grave as resurrected and immortal beings. How could such persons, whose salvation is already assured, possibly be tested? President Joseph Fielding Smith observed that "Satan will be loosed to gather his forces after the millennium. The people who will be tempted, will be people living on this earth [mortals], and they will have every opportunity to accept the gospel or reject it. Satan will have nothing to do whatever with little children, or grown people who have received their resurrection and entered into the celestial kingdom. Satan cannot tempt little children in this life, nor in the spirit world, nor after the resurrection. Little children who die before reaching the years of accountability will not be tempted."[15]

Conclusion

The vision of the celestial kingdom unlocks one of the mysteries of eternity: the blessed concept that the work of the salvation of souls continues after this life is over, well beyond the grave; the work of the Lord goes forward, here and hereafter. We did not first begin to exercise faith in the plan of redemption in this second estate; here and now is but a continuation of there and then. Hereafter we shall continue to labor for ourselves and for our brothers and sisters. Truly, "the course of the Lord is one eternal round" (1 Nephi 10:19).

NOTES

1. Milton V. Backman Jr., *The Heavens Resound: A History of the Latter-day Saints in Ohio* (Salt Lake City: Deseret Book, 1983), 285.

2. Joseph Smith, *History of The Church of Jesus Christ of Latter-day Saints*, ed. B. H. Roberts, 2d ed. rev., 7 vols. (Salt Lake City: Deseret Book, 1957), 2:379–80.

3. Joseph Smith, *Teachings of the Prophet Joseph Smith*, sel. Joseph Fielding Smith (Salt Lake City: Deseret Book, 1976), 347.

4. Smith, *Teachings of the Prophet Joseph Smith*, 367.

5. Smith, *History of the Church*, 5:126.

6. Smith, *History of the Church*, 5:247.

7. Lucy Mack Smith, *History of Joseph Smith by His Mother*, ed. Preston Nibley (Salt Lake City: Bookcraft, 1954), 87.

8. Smith, *History of Joseph Smith*, 88.

9. Smith, *History of the Church*, 5:126–27.

10. Interview with William Smith by E. C. Briggs and J. W. Peterson, in Salt Lake City *Deseret News*, 20 January 1894.
11. Smith, *Teachings of the Prophet Joseph Smith*, 196–97.
12. Bruce R. McConkie, expressing the sentiments of President Joseph Fielding Smith, in "The Salvation of Little Children," *Ensign*, April 1977, 6.
13. Smith, *Teachings of the Prophet Joseph Smith*, 199–200.
14. Joseph F. Smith, *Gospel Doctrine* (Salt Lake City: Deseret Book, 1971), 453.
15. Joseph Fielding Smith, *Doctrines of Salvation*, comp. Bruce R. McConkie, 3 vols. (Salt Lake City: Bookcraft, 1954–56), 2:56–57; see also McConkie, "Salvation of Little Children," 6.

CHAPTER 5

Why Are They Then Baptized for the Dead?

ometime during or just after the mortal ministry of our Lord and Savior, the doctrine of salvation for the dead was revealed to the first-century Church. In chapter 15 of his first epistle to the Corinthians, the apostle Paul testifies of the resurrection of the Lord. Paul presents the core of that supernal message known to us as the gospel, or the "glad tidings" that Christ suffered for our sins, died, rose again the third day, and ascended into heaven. Joseph Smith called these events "the fundamental principles of our religion," to which all other doctrines are but appendages.[1] Paul showed the necessity for the Savior's rising from the tomb and explained that the physical evidence of the divine Sonship of Christ is the resurrection. If Christ had not risen from the dead, Paul asserted, the preaching of the apostles and the faith of the Saints would be in vain. "If in this life only we have hope in Christ," he said, "we are of all men most miserable" (1 Corinthians 15:19).

A PECULIAR DOCTRINE

After establishing that the Lord has conquered all enemies, including death, Paul added: "And when all things shall be subdued unto him, then shall the Son also himself be subject unto him [the Father] that put all things under him, that God may be all in all. Else what shall they do which are baptized for the dead, if the dead rise not at all? why are they then baptized for the dead?" (1 Corinthians 15:28–29). Verse 29 has given rise to a host of interpretations by biblical scholars of various faiths. Many consider the original meaning of the passage to be at best "difficult" or "unclear." One commentator stated that Paul here "alludes to a practice of the Corinthian community as evidence for Christian faith in the resurrection of the dead. It seems that in Corinth some Christians would undergo baptism in the name of their deceased non-Christian relatives and friends, hoping that this vicarious baptism might assure them a share in the redemption of Christ."[2]

Some recent translations of the Bible have attempted to clarify this passage. The New King James Version translates 1 Corinthians 15:29 as "Otherwise, what will they do who are baptized for the dead, if the dead do not rise at all? Why then are they baptized for the dead?" The Revised English Bible translates it as "Again, there are those who receive baptism on behalf of the dead. What do you suppose they are doing? If the dead are not raised to life at all, what do they mean by being baptized on their behalf?" One commentator noted that "it is difficult to imagine any circumstances under which Paul would think it permissible for living Christians to be baptized for the sake of unbelievers in general. Such a view, adopted in part by the Mormons, lies totally outside the NT understanding both of salvation and of baptism."[3]

Indeed, many scholars who are not Latter-day Saints believe that in 1 Corinthians Paul was denouncing or condemning the practice of baptism for the dead as heretical.[4] This is a strange conclusion, because Paul referred to the practice to support the doctrine of the resurrection. In essence, he was asking, "Why are we performing baptism in behalf of our dead, if, as some propose, there will be no resurrection of the dead? If there is to be no resurrection, would not such baptisms be a waste of time?"

One non-Latter-day Saint scholar observed: "Paul had no reason to mention baptism for the dead unless he thought it would be an effective argument with the Corinthians, so presumably he introduced what he thought was an inconsistency in the Corinthians' theology. In this case, some at Corinth might have rejected an afterlife but practiced baptism for the dead, not realizing what the rite implied." In addition, "Because his mention [of the practice] could imply his toleration or approval of it, many have tried to distance Paul from baptism for the dead or remove features regarded as offensive from it. Some maintain that Paul . . . neither approved nor disapproved of the practice by referring to it. Yet it would have been unlike Paul to refrain from criticizing a practice he did not at least tolerate."[5] Or, as Professor Richard L. Anderson pointed out: "Paul was most sensitive to blasphemy and false ceremonialism—of all people he would not have argued for the foundation truth of the resurrection with a questionable example. He obviously did not feel that the principle was disharmonious with the gospel."[6]

In fact, a surprising amount of evidence suggests that the doctrine of salvation for the dead was known and understood by ancient Christian communities. Early commentary on the statement in Hebrews that "they without us should not be made perfect" (Hebrews 11:40) holds that the passage referred to the Old Testament Saints who were trapped in Hades awaiting the help of their New Testament counterparts and that Christ held the keys that would "open the doors of the Underworld to the faithful souls there."[7] It is significant that

59

in his work *Dialogue with Trypho,* Justin Martyr cited an apocryphon that he charged had been deleted from the book of Jeremiah but was still to be found in some synagogue copies of the text: "The Lord God remembered His dead people of Israel who lay in the graves; and He descended to preach to them His own salvation."[8] Irenaeus also taught: "The Lord descended to the parts under the earth, announcing to them also the good news of his coming, there being remission of sins for such as believe on him."[9]

One of the early Christian documents linking the writings of Peter on Christ's ministry in the spirit world (1 Peter 3:18–20; 4:6) with those of Paul on baptism for the dead is *The Shepherd of Hermas,* which states that "these apostles and teachers who preached the name of the Son of God, having fallen asleep in the power and faith of the Son of God, preached also to those who had fallen asleep before them, and themselves gave to them the seal of the preaching. They went down therefore with them into the water and again came up, but the latter went down alive and came up alive, while the former, who had fallen asleep before, went down dead but came up alive. Through them, therefore, they were made alive, and received the knowledge of the name of the Son of God."[10]

A modern commentator on 1 Peter observed that 1 Peter 3:19 and 4:6 are the only passages in the New Testament referring to the ministry of Christ to the postmortal spirit world. "But 1 Peter would not be able," he pointed out, "to make such brief reference to this idea if it were not already known in the churches as tradition. What 1 Peter says in regard to this tradition is, in comparison with the traditions of the second century, quite 'apostolic.'" Through this means, "the saving effectiveness of [the Lord's] suffering unto death extends even to those mortals who in earthly life do not come to a conscious encounter with him, even to the most lost among them."[11]

Tertullian, an early Christian apologist (ca. A.D. 160–240) who later seems to have opposed the practice of baptism for the dead, taught that it was in fact a witness of the bodily resurrection. He quoted Paul's words to the Corinthians and said: "Do not then suppose that the apostle here indicates that some new god is the author and advocate of this practice. Rather, it was so that he could all the more firmly insist upon the resurrection of the body, in proportion of they who are baptized for the dead resorted to the practice from their belief of such a resurrection. We have the apostle in another passage defining 'only one baptism' [Ephesians 4:5]. Therefore, to be 'baptized for the dead' means, in fact, to be baptized for the body. For, as we have shown, it is the body that becomes dead. What, then, will they do who are baptized for the body, if the body does not rise again?"[12] Tertullian declared on another occasion: "Inasmuch as 'some are also baptized for the dead,' we will see whether there is a good reason for this. Now it is certain that they adopted this [practice] with a presumption that made them suppose that the vicarious baptism would be beneficial to the flesh of another in anticipation of the resurrection. For unless this is a bodily resurrection, there would be no pledge secured by this process of a bodily baptism."[13]

LINE UPON LINE

Critics of the practice of baptism for the dead often point out that the practice is nowhere to be found in the Book of Mormon, a scriptural record that contains the "fulness of the gospel of Jesus Christ" (D&C 20:9; 27:5; 42:12; 135:3). We know, of course, that the Book of Mormon is a Christ-centered, gospel-centered volume, focusing repeatedly on the fundamental doctrine of Christ, on what exactly is needed for us to be saved. It does not contain the fulness of gospel doctrine, nor would we expect that all of the theological branches that extend from Christ and the good news of the Atonement would or should be contained within it.

In that regard, we cannot help but appreciate that when the Prophet Joseph Smith learned the gospel, he learned it first and foremost from the Book of Mormon. Later there would be revealed through him, both in his translation of the Bible and through the revelations of the Restoration, ancillary doctrines that would expand his mind and broaden the Saints' understanding of the plan of salvation. What did he learn from the Book of Mormon? He learned that baptism is an essential ordinance, one that must be properly performed to admit a person into the kingdom of God (2 Nephi 31; Mosiah 18). He learned that "this life is the time for men to prepare to meet God; yea, behold the day of this life is the day for men to perform their labors," and that "after this day of life, which is given us to prepare for eternity, behold, if we do not improve our time while in this life, then cometh the night of darkness wherein there can be no labor performed" (Alma 34:32–33). That is to say, in the formative years of his ministry, the Prophet was tutored by the Book of Mormon—a scriptural record that, like Deuteronomy, essentially sets forth the doctrine of the two ways: things are either black or white, good or evil, and our choices lead either to blessing or to cursing.

Sometime between 16 February 1832 and 2 February 1833, Joseph Smith and Sidney Rigdon were involved in the translation of Paul's epistle to the Hebrews. The Prophet rendered verses 39 and 40 as follows: "And these all, having obtained a good report through faith, received not the promises; God having provided some better things for them through their sufferings, for without sufferings they could not be made perfect." The importance of this change—which reflects the context of the chapter on the challenges and trials and sufferings associated with gaining faith unto salvation—is in what it *does not* seem to convey. The King James Version renders the passage thus: "God having provided some better thing for us, that they without us should not be made perfect." The Prophet's alteration of the King James text, an important contribution in its own right, may suggest that at this early date Joseph Smith and the Church did not yet fully grasp the concept of salvation for the dead. If he did, there is no public record of any teachings on the matter at that time.

One of the earliest accounts we have of teachings related to salvation for the dead is found in an experience of Lydia Goldthwait, who later became the wife of Newel Knight. She grew up in Massachusetts and New York and at the age of sixteen married Calvin Bailey. Calvin had a serious drinking problem and eventually left their child and Lydia, who was expecting another baby. The baby died at birth, and within months her first child died also. When she was twenty years old, Lydia moved to Canada to stay with the Freeman Nickerson family. There she was introduced to the restored gospel and first became acquainted with the Prophet Joseph Smith. On 24 October 1833 the family sat around the table and listened to the Prophet. The Spirit was poured out upon the group in a remarkable manner, and Lydia even spoke in tongues.

The next day, as Joseph's company prepared to return to Kirtland, the Prophet "paced back and forth in the sitting room in deep study. Finally he said: 'I have been pondering on Sister Lydia's lonely condition, and wondering why it is that she has passed through so much sorrow and affliction and is thus separated from all her relatives. I now understand it. The Lord has suffered it even as He allowed Joseph of old to be afflicted, who was sold by his brethren as a slave into a far country, and through that became a savior to his father's house and country. Even so shall it be with her, the hand of the Lord will overrule it for good to her and her father's family.'

"Turning to the young girl he continued: 'Sister Lydia, great are your blessings. The Lord, your Savior, loves you, and will overrule all your past sorrows and afflictions for good unto you. Let your heart be comforted. You are of the blood of Israel descended through the loins of Ephraim. You shall yet be a savior to your father's house. Therefore be comforted, and let your heart rejoice, for the Lord has a great work for you to do. Be faithful and endure unto the end and all will be well.'"[14] This statement represents one of the earliest declarations of lineage, as well as one of the first references in this dispensation to individuals becoming what Obadiah called "saviors on mount Zion." As a mature woman, Lydia participated in the ordinance work for some seven hundred of her deceased relatives in the St. George Temple, thus fulfilling Joseph Smith's prophecy.[15]

Joseph Smith's vision of the celestial kingdom (D&C 137), received on 21 January 1836, may well have been the initial revelation of the doctrine of salvation for the dead. Later, on the afternoon of Tuesday, 8 May 1838, the Prophet Joseph answered a series of questions about the faith and practices of the Latter-day Saints. One of the questions was: "If the Mormon doctrine is true, what has become of all those who died since the days of the Apostles?" His response: "All those who have not had an opportunity of hearing the gospel, and being administered to by an inspired man in the flesh, must have it hereafter, before they can be finally judged."[16] We cannot help but conclude that the Prophet must have spoken of this doctrinal matter since the time of his vision of Alvin more than two years earlier, but there is no record of such a conversation.

The first public discourse on the subject by the Prophet was delivered on 15 August 1840 at the funeral of Seymour Brunson, a member of the Nauvoo High Council.[17] Simon Baker described the occasion: "I was present at a discourse that the prophet Joseph delivered on baptism for the dead 15 August 1840. He read the greater part of the 15ᵗʰ chapter of Corinthians and remarked that the Gospel of Jesus Christ brought glad tidings of great joy, and then remarked that he saw a widow in that congregation that had a son who died without being baptized, and this widow in reading the sayings of Jesus 'except a man be born of water and of the spirit he cannot enter the kingdom of heaven,' and that not one jot nor tittle of the Savior's words should pass away, but all should be fulfilled. He then said that this widow should have glad tidings in that thing. He also said the apostle [Paul] was talking to a people who understood baptism for the dead, for it was practiced among them. He went on to say that people could now act for their friends who had departed this life, and that the plan of salvation was calculated to save all who were willing to obey the requirements of the law of God. He went on and made a very beautiful discourse."[18]

After the meeting, the widow, Jane Nyman, was baptized vicariously for her son by Harvey Olmstead in the Mississippi River.[19] Just one month later, on 14 September 1840, on his deathbed the Patriarch Joseph Smith Sr. made a final request of his family—that someone be baptized in behalf of his eldest son, Alvin. Hyrum complied with that wish and was baptized in 1840 and again in 1841.[20]

In an epistle to the Twelve dated 19 October 1840, Joseph Smith stated: "I presume the doctrine of 'baptism for the dead' has ere this reached your ears, and may have raised some inquiries in your minds respecting the same. I cannot in this letter give you all the information you may desire on the subject; but aside from knowledge independent of the Bible, I would say that it was certainly practiced by the ancient churches." The Prophet then quoted from 1 Corinthians 15:29 and continued: "I first mentioned the doctrine in public when preaching the funeral sermon of Brother Seymour Brunson:

and have since then given general instructions in the Church on the subject. The Saints have the privilege of being baptized for those of their relatives who are dead, whom they believe would have embraced the Gospel, if they had been privileged with hearing it, and who have received the Gospel in the spirit, through the instrumentality of those who have been commissioned to preach to them while in prison."[21]

On 19 January 1841 the revelation we know as Doctrine and Covenants 124 was given. In this remarkable oracle the Lord gives a stern warning concerning the need to complete a temple in Nauvoo so that baptisms for the dead may be acceptable before him (D&C 124:29–36). Further, Joseph learned that the ordinance of baptism for the dead was "instituted from before the foundation of the world" (D&C 124:33; compare D&C 128:5, 22).[22] On 3 October 1841 the Prophet declared that baptism for the dead was "the only way that men can appear as saviors on Mount Zion."[23]

On 20 March 1842 the Prophet stated that if we have the authority to perform valid baptisms for the living, it is our responsibility to make those same blessings available to those who have passed through death.[24] On 15 April 1842, in an editorial in the *Times and Seasons,* Joseph the Prophet called upon the Saints to expand their vision beyond the narrow views of unenlightened humankind. "While one portion of the human race are judging and condemning the other without mercy," he said, "the great parent of the universe looks upon the whole of the human family with a fatherly care, and paternal regard; he views them as his offspring; and without any of those contracted feelings that influence the children of men." He observed that "it is an opinion which is generally received, that the destiny of man is irretrievably fixed at his death; and that he is made either eternally happy, or eternally miserable; that if a man dies without a knowledge of God, he must be eternally damned. . . . However orthodox this principle may be, we shall

66

find that it is at variance with the testimony of holy writ; for our Saviour says that all manner of sin, and blasphemy shall be forgiven men wherewith they shall blaspheme; but the blasphemy against the Holy Ghost shall not be forgiven, neither in *this world,* nor in the *world to come,* evidently showing that there are sins which may be forgiven in the *world to come.*" To this doctrinal statement the Prophet added: "The great Jehovah contemplated the whole of the events connected with the earth, pertaining to the plan of salvation, before it rolled into existence, or ever the 'morning stars sung together for joy,' the past, the present and the future, were and are with him, one eternal now." Moreover, Brother Joseph stated, "Chrysostum says that the Marchionites practised baptism for the dead. . . . The church of course at that time was degenerate, and the particular form might be incorrect, but the thing is sufficiently plain in the scriptures." He again quoted 1 Corinthians 15:29 and concluded by referring to the restoration of this vital dimension of the "ancient order of things" as the fulfillment of the words of Obadiah concerning saviors on Mount Zion (Obadiah 1:21). "A view of these things reconciles the scriptures of truth, justifies the ways of God to man; places the human family upon an equal footing, and harmonizes with every principle of righteousness, justice, and truth."[25]

The two epistles to the Church we know as Doctrine and Covenants 127 and 128 contain practical counsel concerning the recording of sacred ordinances (127:5–7; 128:3–4) and also a profound doctrinal foundation upon which we can place those ordinances. Salvation for the dead is a central aspect of the larger work of gathering together all things in one—people as well as principles and precepts—in the dispensation of the fulness of times (D&C 128:15–18). In Doctrine and Covenants 128 the Prophet masterfully blended several scriptural passages in unfolding the doctrinal drama of the Restoration and stated: "These are principles in relation to the dead and the living that

67

cannot be lightly passed over, as pertaining to our salvation." And then, standing in the full light of revealed knowledge concerning these matters, knowledge that he may not yet have possessed at the time of his work on the Bible, he added: "For their salvation is necessary and essential to our salvation, as Paul says concerning the fathers [in Hebrews 11:40]—that they without us cannot be made perfect—neither can we without our dead be made perfect" (D&C 128:15).

On 11 June 1843, while discoursing on the gathering of Israel, Joseph Smith explained that the doctrine of baptism for the dead "was the reason why Jesus said unto the Jews, 'How oft would I have gathered thy children together, even as a hen gathereth her chickens under her wings, and ye would not!'— that they might attend to the ordinances of baptism for the dead as well as other ordinances of the priesthood, and receive revelations from heaven, and be perfected in the things of the kingdom of God—but they would not. This was the case on the day of Pentecost: those blessings were poured out on the disciples on that occasion. God ordained that He would save the dead, and would do it by gathering His people together."[26]

On 7 April 1844, as a part of the King Follett Sermon, Joseph the Seer stated: "I will open your eyes in relation to your dead. All things, which God of his infinite reason has seen fit to reveal to us in our mortal state in regard to our mortal bodies, are revealed to us as if we had no bodies. And those revelations, which will save our dead, will save our bodies. . . . Hence the awful responsibility that rests upon us for our dead, for all the spirits must either obey the gospel or be damned. Solemn thought! Dreadful thought!"[27] According to William Clayton's report, the Prophet also said: "When [God's] commandments teach us, it is in view of eternity. The greatest responsibility in this world is to seek after our dead."[28] One day later the Prophet taught that the temple must be completed "so that men may receive their endowments and be made kings and priests unto the Most High God." The temple, the Prophet continued, "must be built in this central place; for every man who wishes to save his father, mother, brothers, sisters and friends, must go through all the ordinances for each one of them separately, the same as for himself, from baptism to ordination, washing and anointings, and receive all the keys and powers of the Priesthood, the same as for himself."[29]

And then on 2 May 1844 he taught: "In regard to the law of the Priesthood, there should be a place where all nations shall come up from time to time to receive their endowments; and the Lord has said this shall be the place for the baptisms for the dead. Every man that has been baptized and belongs to the kingdom has a right to be baptized for those who have gone before; and as soon as the law of the Gospel is obeyed here by their friends who act as proxy for them, the Lord has administrators there to set them free."[30]

Line upon line, precept upon precept, here a little and there a little the Lord made known significant truths relative to work in behalf of the dead. In time the Saints came to understand, for example, that men should receive the ordinances in behalf of men, women in behalf of women.[31] Some fifty years after the death of the Prophet Joseph Smith, President Wilford Woodruff went before the Lord to seek guidance on a personal matter. In Nauvoo there had grown up a practice among Church members of being "sealed" or "adopted" to prominent Church leaders. And yet there was an unrest, an anxiety among some of the leaders, a quiet realization that the complete mind and will of God had not been made known on the matter. "When I went before the Lord," President Woodruff observed, "to know who I should be adopted to (we were then being adopted to prophets and apostles), the Spirit of God said to me, 'Have you not a father, who begot you?' 'Yes, I have.' 'Then why not honor him? Why not be adopted to him?' 'Yes,' says I, 'that is right.' I was adopted to my father, and should have had my father sealed to his father, and so on back; and the duty that I want every man who presides over a Temple to see performed from this day henceforth and forever, unless the Lord Almighty commands otherwise, is, let every man be adopted to his father." President Woodruff further instructed the Saints: "We want the Latter-day Saints from this time to trace their genealogies as far as they can, and to be sealed to their fathers and mothers. Have children sealed to their parents, and run this chain through as far as you can get it. . . . This is the will of the Lord to his people, and I think when you come to reflect upon it you will find it to be true."³² This divine directive was, of course, fundamental to the establishment of the Genealogical Society and to what we now know as family history associated with the labor of redeeming the dead in temples.

GLAD TIDINGS

The good news or glad tidings of salvation in Christ is intended to lift our sights and bring hope to our souls, to "bind up the brokenhearted, to proclaim liberty to the captives, and the opening of the prison to them that are bound" (Isaiah 61:1). That hope in Christ is in the infinite capacity of an infinite Being to save men and women from ignorance as well as from sin and death. The God of Abraham, Isaac, and Jacob is indeed the God of the living (Matthew 22:32), and his influence and redemptive mercies span the veil of death. The apostle Paul wrote that "if in this life only we have hope in Christ, we are of all men most miserable" (1 Corinthians 15:19).

So what of those who never have the opportunity in this life to know of Christ and his gospel, who never have the opportunity to be baptized for a remission of sins and for entrance into the kingdom of God, who never have the privilege of being bound in marriage and sealed in the family unit? In a world gripped by cynicism and strangled by hopelessness, the scriptures and revelations of the Restoration bear witness of a God of mercy and vision, of an Omnipotent One whose reach to his children is neither blocked by distance nor dimmed by death. And so, after the doctrinal foundation had been laid, God made known through the Prophet of the Restoration those ennobling truths that pertain to life and salvation, both here and hereafter. Truly, as Joseph Smith explained, "It is no more incredible that God should *save* the dead, than that he should *raise* the dead."[33]

In regard to salvation for the dead, the question might well be asked, Then why do missionary work among the living? That is, why send out both young individuals and experienced couples into the world to preach the gospel? Why spend so much money and expend so much time and effort when in fact all people will eventually have the opportunity to hear about the gospel in the world to come? First of all, we go into all the world in an effort to reach every creature because our Lord and Savior has commissioned us to do so (Matthew 28:19–20; Mark 16:15–16; D&C 68:8). But there is always a reason behind what the Lord commands, and so it is with missionary work. We have found one pearl of great price, something worth more than all the silver and all the gold of the earth, and we want to share it with others. As the people of the covenant, those who have come out of the world into the marvelous light of Christ, we desire, with all our hearts, to make those same blessings we enjoy available to all men and women, not only hereafter but here. We don't want people to miss any blessing, any privilege, any joy that could be theirs through the fulness of the gospel. Like Jacob, we seek to "magnify our office unto the Lord, taking upon us the responsibility, answering the sins of the people upon our own heads if we did not teach them the word of God with all diligence" (Jacob 1:19).

71

CONCLUSION

The doctrine of salvation for the dead, the Prophet Joseph declared, "presents in a clear light the wisdom and mercy of God in preparing an ordinance for the salvation of the dead, being baptized by proxy, their names recorded in heaven and they judged according to the deeds done in the body. This doctrine was the burden of the scriptures. Those Saints who neglect it in behalf of their deceased relatives, do it at the peril of their own salvation."[34]

This doctrine and practice, like others centered in the holy temple, links past, present, and future; the living and the dead; time and eternity. It links missionary work on both sides of the veil. "Why is it," Elder Melvin J. Ballard asked, "that sometimes only one of a city or household receives the Gospel?" He answered: "It was made known to me that it is because the righteous dead who have received the Gospel in the spirit world are exercising themselves, and in answers to their prayers elders of the Church are sent to the homes of their posterity so that the Gospel might be taught to them, and that descendant in the flesh is then privileged to do the work for his kindred dead. I want to say to you that it is with greater intensity that the hearts of the fathers and mothers in the spirit world are turned to their children now in the flesh than that our hearts are turned to them."[35] We, the children, thus participate in the realization of the "promises made to the fathers" and thereby help to preserve the earth from destruction (D&C 2:2–3). Surely no work could represent a more noble cause, a more valiant enterprise. And no labor in time could have more eternal implications.

NOTES

1. Joseph Smith, *Teachings of the Prophet Joseph Smith*, sel. Joseph Fielding Smith (Salt Lake City: Deseret Book, 1976), 121.
2. Richard Kugelman, "The First Letter to the Corinthians," in *The Jerome*

Biblical Commentary, ed. Raymond E. Brown, Joseph A. Fitzmyer, and Roland E. Murphy, 2 vols. (Englewood Cliffs, N.J.: Prentice-Hall, 1968), 2:273.

3. Gordon D. Fee, *The First Epistle to the Corinthians* (Grand Rapids, Mich.: Eerdmans, 1987), 767.

4. For a summary of some of the alternative explanations, see Fee, *First Epistle to the Corinthians,* 763–77; see also a more recent proposal in Joel R. White, "'Baptized on Behalf of the Dead,': The Meaning of 1 Corinthians 15:29 in Its Context," *Journal of Biblical Literature* 116, no. 3 (1997): 487–99.

5. Richard E. DeMaris, "Corinthian Religion and Baptism for the Dead (1 Corinthians 15:29): Insights from Archaeology and Anthropology," *Journal of Biblical Literature* 114, no. 4 (1995): 678, 679.

6. Richard L. Anderson, *Understanding Paul* (Salt Lake City: Deseret Book, 1983), 405.

7. J. A. MacCulloch, *The Harrowing of Hell* (Edinburgh, Scotland: T. & T. Clark, 1930), 48–49.

8. MacCulloch, *Harrowing of Hell,* 84–85; *The Ante-Nicene Fathers,* ed. Alexander Roberts and James Donaldson, 10 vols. (Grand Rapids, Mich.: Eerdmans, [1956]), 1:235.

9. Irenaeus, *Against Heresies* 4.27.1, in J. B. Lightfoot, *The Apostolic Fathers* (Grand Rapids, Mich.: Baker Book House, 1962), 277–78.

10. *The Shepherd of Hermas,* in Lightfoot, *Apostolic Fathers,* 232; also in Anderson, *Understanding Paul,* 409.

11. Leonhard Goppelt, *A Commentary on 1 Peter,* ed. Ferdinand Hahn, trans. John E. Alsup (Grand Rapids, Mich.: Eerdmans, 1993), 263, 259.

12. Cited in David W. Bercot, ed., *A Dictionary of Early Christian Beliefs* (Peabody, Mass.: Hendrickson, 1998), 63.

13. Bercot, *Dictionary of Early Christian Beliefs,* 63; Hugh Nibley has surveyed Christian history and traced the practice of baptism for the dead into the Apostasy, during which time it was eventually lost to the world. See Hugh Nibley, *Mormonism and Early Christianity* (Salt Lake City: Deseret Book and F.A.R.M.S., 1987, 100–167), for an enlightening coverage of this fascinating story.

14. "Lydia Knight's History," 21–23, cited in Journal History, 19 October 1833, Church Historian's Office. I am indebted to Professors David Boone and Jeffrey Marsh in Religious Education at BYU for drawing my attention to this story.

15. See *Church History in the Fulness of Times* (Salt Lake City: The Church of Jesus Christ of Latter-day Saints, 1989), 117.

16. In *Elders' Journal* 1, no. 2 (July 1838): 43; Smith, *Teachings of the Prophet Joseph Smith,* 121.

17. Joseph Smith, *History of the Church of Jesus Christ of Latter-day Saints,* ed. B. H. Roberts, 2d ed. rev., 7 vols. (Salt Lake City: Deseret Book, 1957), 4:231.

18. Joseph Smith, *Words of Joseph Smith,* ed. Andrew F. Ehat and Lyndon W. Cook (Provo, Utah: Brigham Young University Religious Studies Center, 1980), 49.

19. From Alex Baugh, "The Practice of Baptism for the Dead Outside of Temples," *Religious Studies Center Newsletter* 13, no. 1 (September 1998): 3–6.

20. "Nauvoo Baptisms for the Dead," Book A, Church Genealogical Society Archives, Salt Lake City, Utah, 145, 149.

21. Smith, *Teachings of the Prophet Joseph Smith,* 179.
22. Smith, *Teachings of the Prophet Joseph Smith,* 308.
23. Smith, *Teachings of the Prophet Joseph Smith,* 191.
24. Smith, *Teachings of the Prophet Joseph Smith,* 201.
25. Smith, *Times and Seasons* 3, no. 12 (15 April 1842): 759–61; Smith, *Teachings of the Prophet Joseph Smith,* 217–23.
26. Smith, *Teachings of the Prophet Joseph Smith,* 310.
27. Smith, *Words of Joseph Smith,* 352; spelling and punctuation standardized.
28. Smith, *Words of Joseph Smith,* 360.
29. Smith, *Teachings of the Prophet Joseph Smith,* 363.
30. Smith, *Teachings of the Prophet Joseph Smith,* 367.
31. See Brigham Young, *Journal of Discourses,* 26 vols. (London: Latter-day Saints' Book Depot, 1851–86), 16:165–66.
32. Wilford Woodruff, Conference Report, April 1894; in Boyd K. Packer, *The Holy Temple* (Salt Lake City: Bookcraft, 1980), 201–2.
33. Smith, *Teachings of the Prophet Joseph Smith,* 191.
34. Smith, *Teachings of the Prophet Joseph Smith,* 193.
35. Melvin J. Ballard, "Three Degrees of Glory," in *Melvin J. Ballard, Crusader for Righteousness* (Salt Lake City: Bookcraft, 1966), 219.

CHAPTER 6

The Redemption of the Dead

I n an address to religious educators in 1977, Elder Boyd K. Packer stressed that we live in a day of great events relating to the scriptures. He reminded us that it had only been a short time since two revelations were added to the standard works, both of which have salvation for the dead as a central theme. Elder Packer continued: "I was surprised, and I think all of the Brethren were surprised, at how casually that announcement of two additions to the standard works was received by the Church. But we will live to sense the significance of it; we will tell our grandchildren and our great-grandchildren, and we will record in our diaries, that we were on the earth and remember when that took place."[1] The two revelations to which Elder Packer referred are Doctrine and Covenants 137 and 138. Having studied the background and significance of the vision of the celestial kingdom (D&C 137), let us now do the same with the vision of the redemption of the dead (D&C 138).

During the last six months of his life, President Joseph F.

Smith suffered from the effects of advancing years (he was in his eightieth year) and spent much of his time in his own room in the Beehive House. President Smith did, however, garner enough strength to attend the eighty-ninth semiannual conference of the Church in October 1918. At the opening session of the conference on Friday, 4 October 1918, he arose to welcome and address the Saints, and said in a voice filled with emotion:

"As most of you, I suppose, are aware, I have undergone a siege of very serious illness for the last five months. It would be impossible for me, on this occasion, to occupy sufficient time to express the desires of my heart and my feelings, as I would desire to express them to you. . . .

"I will not, I dare not, attempt to enter upon many things that are resting upon my mind this morning, and I shall postpone until some future time, the Lord being willing, my attempt to tell you some of the things that are in my mind, and that dwell in my heart. I have not lived alone these last five months. I have dwelt in the spirit of prayer, of supplication, of faith and of determination; and I have had my communication with the Spirit of the Lord continuously."[2]

According to President Smith's son Joseph Fielding Smith, the prophet was expressing, although in broadest terms, the fact that during the past half year he had received numerous manifestations, some of which he shared with his son, both before and after the conference. One of these manifestations, the vision of the redemption of the dead, had been received just the day before, on 3 October, and was recorded immediately following the close of the conference.[3]

PREPARATION FOR THE VISION

At the close of 1916 the Church had 819 wards, 73 stakes, and 21 missions with just over 1,300 full-time missionaries. The Church office building on 47 East South Temple Street was nearing completion, and the first temples outside the continental United States were under construction in Canada and Hawaii.⁴ Two years later the state of the world was cause for serious reflection upon such matters as life and death. World War I, the "war to end all wars," was casting its ominous shadow over the globe, and Latter-day Saints were not immune from its broadening effects. By early January 1919 approximately fifteen thousand members of the Church were serving in the military.⁵ Revolutions in Russia and Finland further intensified anxieties and confirmed fears that war had truly begun to be poured out upon all nations (D&C 87:2). By October of that year an influenza epidemic was spreading throughout the land, leaving death and sorrow in its wake.

Nowhere do we see the critical preparation and readiness for the vision of the redemption of the dead more clearly than in the life and ministry of Joseph F. Smith. The son of Hyrum the Patriarch and nephew of Joseph the Seer, Joseph F. Smith possessed the blood of the prophets. He was foreordained to serve the Lord in the leading councils of the Church and spent the last fifty years of his life realizing that election, actively involved as a legal administrator in the kingdom. He was called while in his teens to serve as a missionary to Hawaii. At age twenty-seven he was called to the apostleship by Brigham Young and served as a counselor in the First Presidency to Presidents Young, Taylor, Woodruff, and Snow before becoming president of the Church in 1901. Intimate associations with the Brethren and personal searchings over several decades distilled and solidified principles and doctrines in the mind of Joseph F. Smith. By the time of his death he had spoken and written upon a myriad of subjects and was a leader well grounded in the theology of the Restoration. One of the greatest compliments paid to President Smith was from President Harold B. Lee. President Lee, himself not shallow in gospel understanding, said, "When I want to seek for a more clear definition of doctrinal subjects, I have usually turned to the writings and sermons of President Joseph F. Smith."[6]

Joseph F.'s attention was drawn to the world beyond mortality by his frequent confrontation with death. His father, Hyrum Smith, was martyred when Joseph F. was a small boy, and his mother, Mary Fielding Smith, died when Joseph F. was thirteen. Of the great trials of his life, none was more devastating than the passing of many of his children into death. President Smith had an almost infinite capacity to love, and the death of loved ones brought extreme anguish and sorrow. Elder Joseph Fielding Smith wrote: "When death invaded his home, as frequently it did, and his little ones were taken from him, he grieved with a broken heart and mourned, not as those mourn who live without hope, but for the loss of his 'precious jewels' dearer to him than life itself."[7]

On 20 January 1918 Hyrum Mack Smith, the eldest son of Joseph F. and a member of the Quorum of the Twelve Apostles, was taken to the hospital for a serious illness. The physicians diagnosed a ruptured appendix. Despite constant medical attention and repeated prayers, Hyrum—then only forty-five years of age and with a pregnant wife—died on the night of 23 January. This was a particularly traumatic affliction for his father. Hyrum Mack had been called as an apostle at the same conference in which his father had been sustained as the sixth president of the Church (October 1901). He was a man of depth and wisdom beyond his years, and his powerful sermons evidenced unusual insight into gospel principles. Elder Heber J. Grant said of him: "In all my travels, week after week, no man of our quorum has ever fed me the bread of life, touched my heart, and caused me to rejoice more in the gospel of Jesus Christ . . . than did our dearly beloved brother whose remains lie before us today. His death comes as a great shock to each and every member of the Council to which he belonged."[8]

President Joseph F. Smith said of his son: "His mind was quick and bright and correct. His judgment was not excelled, and he saw and comprehended things in their true light and meaning. When he spoke, men listened and felt the weight of his thoughts and words." Finally, President Smith observed, "He has thrilled my soul by his power of speech, as no other man ever did. Perhaps this was because he was my son, and he was filled with the fire of the Holy Ghost." Already in a weakened physical condition due to age, the prophet's sudden sense of loss caused him "one of the most severe blows that he was ever called upon to endure." He cried out in anguish: "My soul is rent asunder. My heart is broken, and flutters for life! O my sweet son, my joy, my hope! . . . And now what can I do! O what can I do! My soul is rent, my heart is broken! O God, help me!"[9]

At the funeral service for Elder Smith, Elder James E. Talmage said: "He has gone. Elders are needed on the other side, and apostles of the Lord Jesus Christ are wanted there. . . . I read of the Lord Jesus Christ going, as soon as his spirit left his pierced and tortured body on the cross, to minister unto the spirits on the other side. . . . I cannot think of Hyrum M. Smith as being otherwise employed. I cannot conceive of him as being idle. I cannot think of him having no regard for those among whom he is called to associate.

"And where is he now? . . . [H]e has gone to join the apostles who departed before him, to share with them in the work of declaring the glad message of redemption and salvation unto those who for lack of opportunity, or through neglect, failed to avail themselves of those wondrous and transcendent blessings upon the earth."[10]

An Eventful Thirty Months

President Smith indicated in October 1918 that the preceding six months had been a season of special enrichment.

Indeed, it seems that the last thirty months of his life, from April 1916 to October 1918, represent an era of unusual spiritual enlightenment. At the April 1916 general conference, he gave a remarkable address that established a theme for the rest of his life and ministry and laid the foundation for his final doctrinal contribution—the vision of the redemption of the dead. In his opening sermon, entitled "In the Presence of the Divine," he spoke of the nearness of the world of spirits and of the interest and concern for us and our labors exercised by those who have passed beyond the veil. He stressed that those who labored so diligently in their mortal estate to establish the cause of Zion would not be denied the privilege of "looking down upon the results of their own labors" from their post-mortal estate. In fact, President Smith insisted, "they are as deeply interested in our welfare today, if not with greater capacity, with far more interest, behind the veil, than they were in the flesh." Perhaps the key statement in this sermon was the following: "Sometimes the Lord expands our vision from this point of view and this side of the veil, so that we feel and seem to realize that we can look beyond the thin veil which separates us from that other sphere."[11] That statement, penetrating and prophetic, set the stage for the next two and one-half years.

In June 1916 the First Presidency and the Quorum of the Twelve published a doctrinal exposition in pamphlet form entitled *The Father and the Son*. This document was prepared to alleviate doctrinal misunderstandings concerning the nature of the Godhead and specifically the role and scriptural designation of Jesus Christ as "Father."[12]

Another significant fruit of this time was a talk delivered by President Smith at a fast meeting in the Salt Lake Temple in February 1918, entitled "Status of Children in the Resurrection." This address gives us insight into the power and prophetic stature of one schooled and prepared in doctrine; in addition, we are allowed a brief glimpse into the heart of a noble father who, having lost little ones to death and having mourned their absence, rejoices in the sure knowledge that mortal children are immortal beings, spirits who continue to live and progress beyond the veil, and, as taught by the Prophet Joseph Smith, will come forth from the grave as children and will be nurtured and reared to physical maturity by worthy parents. "O how I have been blessed with these children," exulted President Smith, "and how happy I shall be to meet them on the other side!"[13]

Further evidence of how thin the veil had become for President Joseph F. Smith is found in his recording on 7 April 1918 of a dream he had received many years earlier while on his first mission. The dream had served initially to strengthen the faith and build the confidence of a lonely and weary fifteen-year-old on the slopes of Haleakala on the island of Maui. Through the years that followed, it charted a course for Joseph F. Smith, giving him assurance that his labors were acceptable to the Lord and that he had the approbation of his predecessors in the presidency of the Church. In the dream young Joseph encountered his uncle, the Prophet Joseph, and was fortified in his desire to remain free from the taints of the world. He thus learned at an early age that the separation between mortality and immortality is subtle and that the Lord frequently permits an intermingling of the inhabitants of the two spheres. "That vision, that manifestation and witness that I enjoyed at that time," President Smith. explained, "has made me what I am, if I am anything that is good, or clean, or upright before the Lord, if there is anything good in me. That has helped me out through every trial and through every difficulty." Furthermore, he said, "I know that that was a reality, to show me my duty, to teach me something, and to impress upon me something that I cannot forget."[14]

THE VISION: RECEPTION AND ANNOUNCEMENT

In 1862 President Brigham Young explained that despite the passing of years and the decay of the body, one who opens himself to the realm of divine experience—through loosening his grip upon the here and now—may begin to tighten his grasp upon the things of eternity. "If we live our holy religion and let the Spirit reign," stated President Young, "as the body approaches dissolution the spirit takes a firmer hold on the enduring substance behind the vail, drawing from the depths of that eternal Fountain of Light sparkling gems of intelligence which surround the frail and sinking tabernacle with a halo of immortal wisdom."[15] This poignant principle was beautifully demonstrated in the life of President Joseph F. Smith. Here was a man who met death and sorrow and persecution head on and thus through participating in the fellowship of Christ's suffering was made acquainted with the things of God. A more recent apostle, Elder James E. Faust, explained: "In the agonies of life, we seem to listen better to the faint, godly whisperings of the Divine Shepherd."[16] Of President Smith it was said by Charles W. Nibley, presiding bishop of the Church: "He lived in close communion with the Spirit of the Lord, and his life was so exemplary and chaste that the Lord could easily manifest himself to his servant." Bishop Nibley concluded that "the heart of President Smith was attuned to the Celestial melodies—he could hear, and did hear."[17]

And so, on Thursday, 3 October 1918, President Smith, largely confined to his room because of illness, sat meditating over matters of substance. No doubt because of the world situation, his own suffering, and the loss of loved ones, "he had long pondered the problems connected with making family ties complete in the patriarchal lineages."[18] On this day, the prophet specifically began to read and ponder upon the universal nature of the Atonement and the apostle Peter's allusions to Christ's postmortal ministry. The stage was set: the preparation of a lifetime and the preparation of the moment were recompensed with a heavenly endowment—the vision of the redemption of the dead. President Smith recorded, "As I pondered over these things which are written, the eyes of my understanding were opened, and the Spirit of the Lord rested upon me, and I saw the hosts of the dead, both small and great" (D&C 138:11).

The vision was dictated to his son Joseph Fielding Smith and recorded immediately after the close of the general conference.[19] Interestingly, Elder Smith delivered a discourse entitled "Salvation for the Living and the Dead" at the genealogical conference on the afternoon of Monday, 7 October 1918. There is no mention in this sermon of his father's visionary experience of only four days before, nor are there any of the doctrinal particulars from the vision voiced in the talk. Elder Smith knew well the principle of allowing the prophet the opportunity to deal properly with a matter of new revelation before the contents are put forward to the Church as a whole. On 5 October 1918, in the Saturday afternoon session of conference, President Joseph F. Smith had said simply: "When the Lord reveals something to me, I will consider the matter with my brethren, and when it becomes proper, I will let it be known to the people, and not otherwise."[20]

President Smith saw fit to consider the matter of the vision in the Thursday Council Meeting of 31 October. Because of his weakened condition, the President did not attend but asked his son Joseph Fielding Smith to present the vision to the combined gathering of the counselors in the First Presidency, the Quorum of the Twelve Apostles, and the Patriarch to the Church. President Anthon H. Lund, first counselor to President Smith, recorded: "In our Council Joseph F. Smith Jr. read a revelation which his father had had in which he saw

83

the spirits in Paradise and he also saw that Jesus organized a number of brethren to go and preach to the spirits in prison, but did not go himself. It was an interesting document and the apostles accepted it as true and from God."[21] Elder James E. Talmage of the Council of the Twelve recorded the following in his journal regarding this occasion: "Attended meeting of the First Presidency and the Twelve. Today President Smith who is still confined to his home by illness, sent to the Brethren an account of a vision through which, as he states, were revealed to him important facts relating to the work of the disembodied Savior in the realm of departed spirits, and of the missionary work in progress on the other side of the veil. By united action the Council of the Twelve, with the Counselors in the First Presidency, and the Presiding Patriarch accepted and endorsed the revelation as the Word of the Lord. President Smith's signed statement will be published in the next issue (December) of the *Improvement Era*, which is the organ of the Priesthood quorums of the Church."[22] The text of the vision first appeared in the 30 November 1918 edition of the *Deseret News*, and it was then printed in the December *Improvement Era* and in the January 1919 issues of the *Relief Society Magazine*, the *Utah Genealogical and Historical Magazine*, the *Young Women's Journal*, and the *Millennial Star*.

President Smith's physical condition worsened during the first weeks of November 1918. On Sunday, 17 November 1918, he was taken with an attack of pleurisy, which finally developed into pleuropneumonia. Tuesday morning 19 November 1918, his work in mortality was completed. At the general conference held in June 1919, Elder James E. Talmage delivered the following tribute to President Smith: "He was permitted shortly before his passing to have a glimpse into the hereafter, and to learn where he would soon be at work. He was a preacher of righteousness on earth, he is a preacher of righteousness today. He was a missionary from his boyhood

84

up, and he is a missionary today amongst those who have not yet heard the gospel, though they have passed from mortality into the spirit world. I cannot conceive of him as otherwise than busily engaged in the work of the Master."[23]

DOCTRINAL SIGNIFICANCE

The vision of the redemption of the dead is central to the theology of the Latter-day Saints. It confirms and expands upon earlier prophetic insights concerning work for the dead, and it introduces doctrinal truths not had in the Church before October 1918.

While pondering upon the infinite atonement of Christ and particularly upon Peter's testimony of the same in the third and fourth chapters of Peter's first epistle, President Joseph F. Smith was enlightened by the Spirit and power of God. He saw within the veil and viewed the proceedings within the world of spirits (D&C 138:1–11). He first saw "an innumerable company of the spirits of the just," that is to say, the righteous dead in paradise from the days of Adam to the meridian of time (D&C 138:12). They were anxiously awaiting the advent of the Christ into their dimension of life and were exuberant in their joy over an imminent resurrection (D&C 138:13–17). Having consummated the atoning sacrifice on Golgotha, the Lord of the living and the dead passed in the twinkling of an eye into the world of the departed. The dead, having "looked upon the long absence of their spirits from their bodies as a bondage," are in a sense in prison (D&C 138:50; see also D&C 45:17). Yes, even the righteous seek "deliverance" (D&C 138:15); the Master came to declare "liberty to the captives who had been faithful" (D&C 138:18). As Peter said, Christ went beyond the veil to preach "unto the spirits in prison" (1 Peter 3:19). Elder Bruce R. McConkie explained that in the vision "it is clearly set forth that the

85

whole spirit world, and not only that portion designated as hell, is considered to be a spirit prison."[24]

The Lord appeared to the congregation of the righteous, and "their countenances shone, and the radiance from the presence of the Lord rested upon them" (D&C 138:24). President Smith observed the Lord teaching "the everlasting gospel, the doctrine of the resurrection and the redemption of mankind from the fall, and from individual sins on conditions of repentance" (D&C 138:19). In addition, Christ extended to the righteous spirits "power to come forth, after his resurrection from the dead, to enter into his Father's kingdom, there to be crowned with immortality and eternal life" (D&C 138:51).

While pondering the question of how the Savior could have taught the gospel to so many in the spirit world in so short a time, perhaps no more than thirty-eight to forty hours, President Smith received what may be the most significant doctrinal insight of the entire vision. The prophet understood "that the Lord went not in person among the wicked and disobedient"—those in hell, or outer darkness—but rather "organized his forces and appointed messengers, clothed with power and authority," that such representatives might carry the message of the gospel "unto whom he [the Lord] could not go personally, because of their rebellion and transgression" (D&C 138:20–22, 25–30, 37). Christ's mission to the world of spirits was thus as much organizational as instructional. The chosen messengers declared "the acceptable day of the Lord" (D&C 138:31). They carried the gospel message to those who had had no opportunity in mortality to accept or reject the truth and also to those who had rejected the message on earth. Those who were visited by the messengers were taught the first principles and ordinances of the gospel, including vicarious ordinances, so that they might be judged and rewarded by the same divine standards as those who inhabit the world of mortals (D&C 138:31–34).

In this vision the Lord saw fit to add "line upon line, pre-cept upon precept" to the understanding of the Latter-day Saints relative to the work of redemption beyond the grave (D&C 98:12). It appears the insight that Christ did not person-ally visit the disobedient is a doctrinal matter introduced to the Church for the first time in 1918. It does much to broaden our scope and answer questions with regard to the work within that sphere. Elder Orson F. Whitney wrote in the 20 February 1919 issue of the *Millennial Star*: "The new light here thrown upon the subject proceeds from the declaration that when the Savior visited the inhabitants of the Spirit World, it was by proxy and not in person so far as the wicked were concerned. He ministered to the righteous directly, and to the unrighteous indirectly, sending to them His servants bearing the authority of the Priesthood and duly commissioned to speak and act in His name and stead. President Smith's pronouncement is a modification of the view commonly taken, that the Savior's personal ministry was to both classes of spirits."[25]

President Smith's pronouncement as a "modification of the view commonly taken" is evident if we note that in a major doctrinal standard, *Jesus the Christ*, first published three years earlier, in 1915, Elder Talmage had taken a traditional approach to the subject.[26] The revolutionary and inspiring nature of this particular contribution is also manifest in the fact that President Smith himself had taught on previous occa-sions of Christ's postmortal ministry to the wicked and unbe-lieving.[27] In this sense the doctrine was truly a "revelation" to the prophet as well as to the people.

President Smith beheld that "the chosen messengers went forth to declare the acceptable day of the Lord and proclaim liberty to the captives who were bound, even unto all who would repent of their sins and receive the gospel. Thus was the gospel preached to those who had died in their sins, without a knowledge of the truth" (D&C 138:31–32). We learn in the vision of the celestial kingdom that those who had not had the opportunity to receive the gospel but who would have done so had they been granted that opportunity are heirs of the celestial kingdom (D&C 137:7–9). But the new knowledge we are given here pertains to the fact that President Smith also witnessed the preaching of the gospel to those "in transgression, having rejected the prophets" (D&C 138:31–32).

Often factors in this life bear upon a person's capacity to recognize and cleave unto the truth. Surely in the postmortal spirit world, such burdens as that of abuse, neglect, false teachings, and improper traditions—any of which can deter one from embracing the truth—will be lifted. Then perhaps they will in that sphere, free from Lucifer's taunts, see as they are seen and know as they are known. President Wilford Woodruff stated: "I tell you when the prophets and apostles go to preach to those who are shut up in prison, thousands of them will there embrace the Gospel. They know more in that world than they do here."[28] President Lorenzo Snow also pointed out: "Within the last few months thousands of people in the spirit world have been placed in a condition that they may receive the word of God and be saved, through the ordinances that have been administered in these four temples in this Territory. A wonderful work is being accomplished in our temples in favor of the spirits in prison. I believe, strongly too, that when the Gospel is preached to the spirits in prison, the success attending that preaching will be far greater than that attending the preaching of our Elders in this life. I believe there will be very few indeed of those spirits who will not gladly receive the Gospel when it is carried to them. The circumstances there will be a thousand times more favorable. . . . I believe there will be very few who will not receive the truth. They will hear the voice of the Son of God; they will hear the voice of the Priesthood of the Son of God, and they will receive the truth and live."[29]

By the power of the Holy Ghost President Smith perceived the identity of many of the noble and great ones from the beginning of time, including Adam, Seth, Noah, Abraham, Isaiah, the Nephite prophets before Christ, and many more. In addition, the prophet recognized Mother Eve and many of her faithful daughters. President Smith had taught for several years concerning the labors of women in the spirit world (D&C 138:38–49).[30]

Verses 53 and 54 are particularly fascinating: "The Prophet Joseph Smith, and my father, Hyrum Smith, Brigham Young, John Taylor, Wilford Woodruff, and other choice spirits who were reserved to come forth in the fulness of times to take part in laying the foundations of the great latter-day work, including the building of the temples and the performance of ordinances therein for the redemption of the dead, were also in the spirit world." These verses have given rise to the idea among some Church members that the premortal spirit world and the postmortal spirit world are joined somehow and that there is an intermingling of those who have died with those who are yet to be born. Though there does not seem to be any authoritative statement to that effect or, indeed, any prophetic commentary on the matter, surely it would have been appropriate for many of the faithful in their premortal existence to be allowed to enter the postmortal spirit world to witness the ministry of the Divine Redeemer to the disembodied.

It may be also that the vision at this point shifts in time— from a gathering of workers from the first century after Christ to a gathering of workers in the spirit world during the final dispensation. A shift in time frame is common in visions, as can be seen from the experiences of Nephi (1 Nephi 13–14), John the Apostle (Revelation 11–12), and Joseph Smith (D&C 76). President Smith could have been permitted to witness the postmortal labors of his predecessors in the presidency of the restored Church, to glimpse that world where he would soon be at work.

President Joseph F. Smith's vision confirms another doctrine that had been taught by Joseph Smith—that the faithful in this life continue to teach and labor in the world of spirits in behalf of those who did not know God. As recorded in George Laub's journal under the date of 12 May 1844 the Prophet Joseph proclaimed: "Now all those [who] die in the faith go to the prison of Spirits to preach to the dead in body, but they are alive in the Spirit, and those Spirits preach to the Spirits that they may live according to God in the Spirit and men do minister for them in the flesh."[31] President Joseph F. Smith had himself taught this doctrine on a number of occasions;[32] here he became an eyewitness of the same.

President Smith then reconfirmed the law concerning the dead and the preaching of the gospel. Gaining salvation is by individual decision, and God will force exaltation upon no man. Those spirits who repent and accept the gospel and the ordinances performed vicariously in their behalf "shall receive a reward according to their works, for they are heirs of salvation" (D&C 138:59; see also vv. 31, 58).[33]

Having laid out his remarkable vision—"a complete and comprehensive confirmation of the established doctrine of the church where salvation for the dead is concerned"[34]— President Joseph F. Smith concluded his doctrinal contribution with a testimony: "Thus was the vision of the redemption of the dead revealed to me, and I bear record, and I know that this record is true, through the blessing of our Lord and Savior, Jesus Christ, even so. Amen" (D&C 138:60).

FROM REVELATION TO CANONIZED SCRIPTURE

In 1919 the writings and sermons of President Joseph F. Smith were compiled and published under the title *Gospel*

Doctrine, a work intended originally as a course of study for Melchizedek Priesthood quorums. The vision of the redemption of the dead was contained in that volume as chapter 24 and entitled "Eternal Life and Salvation." The vision was therefore available to those Saints who made *Gospel Doctrine* a part of their Church library or who turned to the book in their doctrinal studies.

In the afternoon session of conference on Saturday, 3 April 1976, President N. Eldon Tanner made the following announcement: "President Kimball has asked me to read a very important resolution for your sustaining vote.

"At a meeting of the Council of the First Presidency and the Quorum of the Twelve held in the Salt Lake Temple on March 25, 1976, approval was given to add to the Pearl of Great Price the two following revelations:

"First, a vision of the celestial kingdom given to Joseph Smith the Prophet in the Kirtland Temple, on January 21, 1836, which deals with the salvation of those who die without a knowledge of the Gospel; second, a vision given to President Joseph F. Smith in Salt Lake City, Utah, on October 3, 1918, showing the visit of the Lord Jesus Christ in the spirit world, and setting forth the doctrine of the redemption of the dead.

"It is proposed that we sustain and approve this action and adopt these revelations as part of the standard works of the Church of Jesus Christ of Latter-day Saints.

"All those in favor manifest it. Those opposed, if any, by the same sign.

"Thank you. President Kimball, the voting seems to be unanimous in the affirmative."[35]

The vision of the redemption of the dead thus became a part of the standard works, specifically, an addition to the Pearl of Great Price.[36] The First Presidency and the Twelve had discussed including these two revelations in the standard works on a number of occasions before March 1976. Elder Bruce R. McConkie, a member of the Twelve, divided the two visions into verses, as we now have them. In a letter regarding the canonization of President Joseph F. Smith's vision, Elder McConkie explained: "President Kimball and all the Brethren thought it should be formally and officially recognized as scripture so that it would be quoted, used, and relied upon more than the case would have been if it had simply been published as heretofore in various books. By putting it in the Standard Works formally, it gets cross referenced and is used to better advantage by the Saints."[37]

Taking the lead in quoting and relying on these revelations, President Spencer W. Kimball did a most unusual and impressive thing not long after the vision was added to the collection of holy writ. In a meeting with the general authorities and regional representatives of the Twelve, he read the entire text of the vision of the redemption of the dead as part of his own address.[38] In June 1979 by administrative decision and "as a very direct outgrowth of the [new] scripture project,"[39] the two revelations approved in April 1976 were shifted to the Doctrine and Covenants, becoming sections 137 and 138, respectively.[40]

CONCLUSION

There can be no doubt that the vision of the redemption of the dead was scripture before 3 April 1976; it was certainly spoken by the power of the Holy Ghost, and it represented the will, mind, word, and voice of the Lord (D&C 68:4). In 1918 the First Presidency, Quorum of the Twelve, and Patriarch to the Church recognized and acknowledged it as "true and from God." Once it had been voted upon and accepted by the membership of the Church, however, it moved from scripture to canonized scripture. Before 3 April 1976 it represented a theological document of significant worth to the Saints, one that deserved the study of those interested in spiritual things; on the date it was accepted into the standard works, its message—principles and doctrines—became binding[41] upon the Latter-day Saints, the same as the revelations of Moses or Jesus or Alma or Joseph Smith. The vision of the redemption of the dead became a part of the canon, the rule of faith and doctrine and practice—the written measure by which we discern truth from error.

In a day when the First Presidency has specifically defined the mission of the Church and specified that that mission—which is to invite all to come unto Christ—is to be accomplished through proclaiming the gospel, perfecting the Saints, and redeeming the dead, it seems fitting that we focus greater attention upon a significant revelation that provides a spiritual justification for the Church's continued expansion in family history and temple work. President Joseph F. Smith's vision has expanded our vision "from this point of view and on this side of the veil," so that now, better than ever before, "we can look beyond the thin veil which separates us from that other sphere."[42]

NOTES

1. Boyd K. Packer, "Teach the Scriptures," address delivered to Church Educational System personnel, 14 October 1977, Salt Lake City; in *Charge to Religious Educators*, 2d ed. (Salt Lake City: The Church of Jesus Christ of Latter-day Saints, 1981), 21.

2. Joseph F. Smith, Conference Report, October 1918, 2. In reporting the address, the *Improvement Era* (November 1918, 80) recorded: "He was visibly affected when he arose to make his opening speech which was listened to with profound silence."

3. Joseph Fielding Smith, *The Life of Joseph F. Smith* (Salt Lake City: Deseret Book, 1969), 466.

4. Joseph F. Smith, Conference Report, April 1917, 8–9.

5. In Joseph Fielding Smith, *Essentials in Church History* (Salt Lake City: Deseret Book, 1967), 516–17.

6. Harold B. Lee, Conference Report, October 1972, 18.

7. Smith, *Life of Joseph F. Smith*, 455.

8. Heber J. Grant, in "In Memoriam: Hyrum Mack Smith," *Improvement Era*, March 1918, 380.

9. Smith, *Life of Joseph F. Smith,* 474.

10. James E. Talmage, *Improvement Era,* March 1918, 384.

11. Joseph F. Smith, Conference Report, April 1916, 2.

12. First Presidency and Quorum of the Twelve Apostles, *Improvement Era,* August 1916, 934–42; *Messages of the First Presidency of The Church of Jesus Christ of Latter-day Saints,* comp. James R. Clark, 6 vols. (Salt Lake City: Bookcraft, 1965–75), 5:23–34.

13. Joseph F. Smith, *Improvement Era,* May 1918, 570; Clark, *Messages of the First Presidency,* 5:90–98.

14. Joseph F. Smith, *Improvement Era,* November 1919, 16–17; Clark, *Messages of the First Presidency,* 5:99–101; Smith, *Life of Joseph F. Smith,* 445–47.

15. Brigham Young, *Journal of Discourses,* 26 vols. (London: Latter-day Saints' Book Depot, 1851–86), 9:288.

16. James E. Faust, Conference Report, April 1979, 77.

17. Charles W. Nibley, *Improvement Era,* January 1919, 197–98.

18. "Family Life, An Eternal Unit—Joseph F. Smith," *Relief Society Magazine,* January 1941, 57.

19. Joseph Fielding Smith, in his biography of his father, stated that Joseph F. Smith saw to it that the vision was "written immediately following the close of that conference" (*Life of Joseph F. Smith,* 466). Joseph Fielding Smith Jr. and John J. Stewart, in their biography of Joseph Fielding Smith, wrote: "This vision [Joseph F.] received on October 3, 1918, the day before General Conference convened. Two weeks later Joseph Fielding wrote the vision as his father dictated it to him" (*The Life of Joseph Fielding Smith* [Salt Lake City: Deseret Book, 1972], 201).

20. Joseph F. Smith, Conference Report, October 1918, 57.

21. Anthon H. Lund Journal, LDS Church Archives, Salt Lake City, Utah, 31 October 1918.

22. James E. Talmage Journal, Harold B. Lee Library, Brigham Young University, Provo, Utah, 31 October 1918.

23. James E. Talmage, Conference Report, June 1919, 60.

24. Bruce R. McConkie, "A New Commandment: Save Thyself and Thy Kindred!" *Ensign,* August 1976, 11.

25. Orson F. Whitney, *The Latter-day Saints' Millennial Star* 8, no. 81 (20 February 1919): 116.

26. James E. Talmage, "The Living and the Dead," *Utah Genealogical and Historical Magazine,* July 1918, 126. The article states the following: "While in the bodiless state our Lord ministered among the departed, both in Paradise and in the prison realm where dwelt in a state of durance the spirits of the disobedient." See also James E. Talmage, *Jesus the Christ* (Salt Lake City: Deseret Book, 1972), 672.

27. Joseph F. Smith quoted first from Peter's epistle and then remarked: "This may seem strange to some, that Jesus should go to preach the Gospel unto the wicked, rebellious antediluvians, . . . nevertheless it is true." In the same sermon, he said: "Thus we see those wicked, unrepentant antediluvians who even had the privilege of hearing the Gospel in the flesh, as preached by Noah, . . . were actually visited in the 'prison house' by the Savior himself, and heard the Gospel from his own mouth after he was 'put to death in the

flesh'" (*Journal of Discourses*, 18:92). See also Joseph F. Smith, "Redemption beyond the Grave," *Improvement Era*, December 1901, 145–47.

28. Wilford Woodruff, cited in Boyd K. Packer, *The Holy Temple* (Salt Lake City: Bookcraft, 1980), 206.

29. Lorenzo Snow, in *Collected Discourses: Delivered by President Wilford Woodruff, His Two Counselors, The Twelve Apostles, and Others*, comp. Brian H. Stuy, 5 vols. (Sandy, Utah: BHS Publishing, 1987–92), 3:363.

30. Joseph F. Smith, *Young Women's Journal* 23, no. 3 (1911): 128–32; *Gospel Doctrine* (Salt Lake City: Deseret Book, 1971), 461.

31. Joseph Smith, *Words of Joseph Smith*, comp. Andrew F. Ehat and Lyndon W. Cook (Provo: Brigham Young University Religious Studies Center, 1980), 370; spelling and punctuation standardized. From the Samuel W. Richards Record: "The sectarians have no charity for me but I have for them. I intend to send men to prison to preach to them" (Smith, *Words of Joseph Smith*, 371).

32. See, for example, Smith, *Gospel Doctrine*, 134–35, 460–61.

33. Joseph Fielding Smith taught that Christ, in the meridian of time, "bridged the gulf" between paradise and hell, or outer darkness (cf. Luke 16:26): "From that time forth this gulf is bridged so that the captives, after they have paid the full penalty of their misdeeds, satisfied justice, and have accepted the gospel of Christ, having the ordinances attended to in their behalf by their living relatives or friends, receive the passport that entitles them to cross the gulf" (*Doctrines of Salvation*, comp. Bruce R. McConkie, 3 vols. [Salt Lake City: Bookcraft, 1954–56], 2:185).

34. McConkie, "New Commandment," 11.

35. N. Eldon Tanner, Conference Report, April 1976, p. 29.

36. Elder Boyd K. Packer said: "We live in a day of great events relating to the scriptures. It has been only a short time, something more than a year, since two revelations were added to the scriptures, to the standard works, both of these to the Pearl of Great Price. Some have asked, 'Why did they go in the Pearl of Great Price? Why not the Doctrine and Covenants?' They could have gone either place; they were put in the Pearl of Great Price" (address to CES personnel, 14 October 1977).

37. Bruce R. McConkie to Robert L. Millet, 5 October 1983.

38. Spencer W. Kimball, address to Regional Representatives' seminar, 30 September 1977.

39. Boyd K. Packer, Conference Report, October 1982, 75–76. Elder Bruce R. McConkie stated: "As to whether it [the vision of the redemption of the dead] should be in the Pearl of Great Price or the Doctrine and Covenants, that is simply an administrative decision. A number of our revelations have been published in both places over the years. It seems to me that it is properly placed in the Doctrine and Covenants" (letter to Robert L. Millet, 5 October 1983).

40. "Additions to D&C Approved," *Church News*, 2 June 1979, 3.

41. McConkie, "New Commandment," 7.

42. Joseph F. Smith, Conference Report, April 1916, 2.

CHAPTER 7

Exaltation and Eternal Life

Elder Bruce R. McConkie observed: "There was not so much as the twinkling of an eye during the whole so-called pre-Christian era when the Church of Jesus Christ was not upon the earth, organized basically in the same way it now is. . . . There was always apostolic power. The Melchizedek Priesthood always directed the course of the Aaronic Priesthood. All of the prophets held a position in the hierarchy of the day. Celestial marriage has always existed. Indeed, such is the heart and core of the Abrahamic covenant. Elias and Elijah came to restore this ancient order and to give the sealing power, which gives it eternal efficacy."[1]

THE KEYS OF THE PRIESTHOOD RESTORED

The winter and spring of 1836 proved to be an era of both modern Pentecost and modern transfiguration. By early April, bearers of the priesthood had been washed and anointed. On

Sunday, 3 April 1836, one week after the first dedicatory service of the Kirtland Temple, the Saints were again assembled in the house of the Lord. In the morning Elder Thomas B. Marsh, then president of the Quorum of the Twelve Apostles, and Elder David W. Patten were called upon to speak. In the afternoon the First Presidency and the apostles participated in a sacrament service, after which Joseph Smith and Oliver Cowdery knelt in prayer behind drawn curtains near the large pulpits on the west side of the main floor of the temple. At that moment a wondrous vision burst upon them, one of the most significant theophanies of the ages.

Jesus the Christ appeared. Our Lord's appearance was the beginning of the realization of his promise given three years earlier: "And inasmuch as my people build a house unto me in the name of the Lord, and do not suffer any unclean thing to come into it, that it be not defiled, my glory shall rest upon it; yea, and my presence shall be there, for I will come into it, and all the pure in heart that shall come into it shall see God" (D&C 97:15–16). The Savior accepted the offering of his Saints—this temple built at great sacrifice—and then expanded their vision of the importance of what they had accomplished: "Yea the hearts of thousands and tens of thousands shall greatly rejoice in consequence of the blessings which shall be poured out, and the endowment with which my servants have been endowed in this house" (D&C 110:9).

"After this vision [of the Savior] closed, the heavens were again opened unto us; and Moses appeared before us, and committed unto us the keys of the gathering of Israel from the four parts of the earth, and the leading of the ten tribes from the land of the north" (D&C 110:11). The keys, or directing powers, restored by the ancient Lawgiver formalized the work of gathering that had begun earlier. These keys enabled the Saints to accomplish the directive delivered in September 1830: "And ye are called to bring to pass the gathering of mine elect; for mine elect hear my voice and harden not their hearts" (D&C 29:7). To the president of The Church of Jesus Christ of Latter-day Saints—the man appointed "to preside over the whole church, and to be like unto Moses" (D&C 107:91)—were given keys to gather modern Israel. Even as Moses led ancient Israel out of Egyptian bondage, so the president of the Church was given keys to lead modern Israel out of the bondage of modern Egypt into Zion.

"After this, Elias appeared, and committed the dispensation of the gospel of Abraham, saying that in us and our seed all generations after us should be blessed" (D&C 110:12). The identity of Elias is not given in the revelation, but this heavenly messenger restored the keys necessary to establish the ancient patriarchal order, making Joseph Smith and the faithful Saints who receive celestial marriage heirs to the blessings and "promises made to the fathers"—Abraham, Isaac, and Jacob. Elias thus restored the power by which eternal families are organized through the new and everlasting covenant of marriage. "As the crowning cause for wonderment," Elder Bruce R. McConkie explained, "that God who is no respecter of persons has given a like promise [to that of Abraham and Joseph Smith] to every [member] in the kingdom who has gone to the holy temple and entered into the blessed order of matrimony there performed. Every person married in the temple for time and for all eternity has sealed upon him, conditioned upon his faithfulness, all of the blessings of the ancient patriarchs, including the crowning promise and assurance of eternal increase, which means, literally, a posterity as numerous as the dust particles of the earth."[2]

"After this vision had closed, another great and glorious vision burst upon us; for Elijah the prophet, who was taken to heaven without tasting death, stood before us, and said: Behold, the time has fully come, which was spoken of by the mouth of Malachi—testifying that he [Elijah] should be sent, before the great and dreadful day of the Lord come—to turn the hearts of the fathers to the children, and the children to the fathers, lest the whole earth be smitten with a curse" (D&C 110:13–15). Precisely on the day that Elijah's appearance took place, Jews throughout the world were engaged in celebrating the Passover. Since the time of Malachi, from about 400 or 500 B.C. until now, Jews worldwide have awaited Elijah's coming with anxious anticipation. Elijah did come, but not to Jewish homes; he came rather to a synagogue of the Saints and to Christ's legal administrators on earth. There he bestowed keys of inestimable worth.

When Moroni appeared to Joseph Smith in 1823 he quoted numerous passages from the Old and New Testaments. The Prophet indicated in his official history that Moroni quoted Malachi 4:5–6 but gave a rendering different from that in the King James Version. Malachi (through whom this promise came), we learn from the Prophet, "had his eye fixed on the restoration of the priesthood" (D&C 128:17). The prophecy began: "Behold, I will reveal unto you the Priesthood, by the hand of Elijah the prophet, before the coming of the great and dreadful day of the Lord" (Joseph Smith–History 1:38; D&C 2:1). Joseph Smith and Oliver Cowdery had been ordained to the Melchizedek Priesthood and given apostolic power and commission as early as 1829. How was it, then, that Elijah would *reveal* the priesthood? Simply stated, Elijah was sent in 1836 to reveal, or make known, keys of the priesthood and sealing powers that had not yet been fully understood or were not fully operational in this dispensation, especially in regard to families. Now the power to gather, organize, and seal families was fully functional. Elijah restored the keys whereby families, organized in the patriarchal order through the powers delivered by Elias, could be bound and sealed for eternity.

Three months before his death, Joseph Smith instructed

the Latter-day Saints concerning the mission of Elijah: "The spirit, power, and calling of Elijah is, that ye have power to hold the key of the revelations, ordinances, oracles, powers and endowments of the fulness of the Melchizedek Priesthood and of the kingdom of God on the earth."[3] Elijah restored the keys whereby individuals and families may, through the blessings of the holy temple, develop line upon line to the point where they receive the fulness of the priesthood and thus become kings and queens, priests and priestesses unto God in the patriarchal order.[4] Through the powers delivered by Elias—the new and everlasting covenant of marriage, the order entered into by Abraham, Isaac, and Jacob—eternal families are created, here and hereafter. Through the powers delivered by Elijah, husband and wife may be sealed unto eternal life, inasmuch as "the power of Elijah is sufficient to make our calling and election sure."[5]

Elijah came to "plant in the hearts of the children the promises made to the fathers" whereby the "hearts of the children [should] turn to their fathers" (Joseph Smith–History 1:39; D&C 2:2). The Spirit of the Lord witnesses to faithful Latter-day Saints of the central place of eternal marriage and of the sublime joys associated with the everlasting continuation of the family. Through temples, God's promises to the fathers—the promises pertaining to the gospel, the priesthood, and eternal increase (Abraham 2:8–11)—are extended to all faithful Saints of all the ages. The hearts of the children turn to the ancient fathers because the children are now participants in and recipients of the blessings of the fathers. Being profoundly grateful for such privileges, members of the Church, motivated by the Spirit of Elijah, also find their hearts turning to their more immediate fathers and do all within their power, through family history research and attendant temple work, to ensure that the blessings of Abraham, Isaac, and Jacob are enjoyed by their ancestry as well as their posterity. "If it were not so [that is, if Elijah had not come], the whole earth would be utterly wasted at [Christ's] coming" (Joseph Smith–History 1:39; D&C 2:3).

Why? Because the earth would not have accomplished its foreordained purpose: to establish on its face a family system patterned after the order of heaven. If there were no sealing powers whereby families could be bound together, then the earth would never "answer the end of its creation" (D&C 49:16). It would be wasted and cursed, for all men and women would be forever without root or branch, without ancestry or posterity. Because Elijah came, however, all ordinances for the living and the dead (baptisms, confirmations, ordinations, sealings, and so on) have real meaning and are of efficacy, virtue, and force in eternity.[6] The ordinances associated with the ministry and bestowal of keys by Moses, Elias, and Elijah, culminating in temples of the Lord, are the capstone blessings of the gospel and the consummation of the Father's work: they provide purpose and perspective for all other gospel principles and ordinances.

In summary, as President Ezra Taft Benson explained: "Elijah brought the keys of sealing powers—that power which *seals* a man to a woman and *seals* their posterity to them endlessly, that which *seals* their forefathers to them all the way back to Adam. This is the power and order that Elijah revealed—that *same order* of priesthood which God gave to Adam and to all the ancient patriarchs which followed after him."[7] Elder James E. Faust pointed out: "Perhaps we regard the power bestowed by Elijah as something associated only with formal ordinances performed in sacred places. But these ordinances become dynamic and productive of good only as they reveal themselves in our daily lives. Malachi said that the power of Elijah would turn the *hearts* of the fathers and the children to each other. The heart is the seat of the emotions and a conduit for revelation (see Malachi 4:5–6). This sealing power thus reveals itself in family relationships, in attributes and virtues developed in a nurturing environment, and in loving service. These are the cords that bind families together, and the priesthood advances their development."[8]

Ours is the day of restitution. Into the ocean of our dispensation flow the rivers and streams of dispensations past. It is necessary in our day and in a time yet future "that a whole and complete and perfect union, and welding together of dispensations, and keys, and powers, and glories should take place, and be revealed from the days of Adam even to the present time. And not only this, but those things which never have been revealed from the foundation of the world, but have been kept hid from the wise and prudent, shall be revealed unto babes and sucklings in this, the dispensation of the fulness of times" (D&C 128:18; compare 112:30–31). The keys of the kingdom of God—restored by such heavenly messengers as John the Baptist, Peter, James, John, Moses, Elias, Elijah, Michael, Raphael, and divers angels (D&C 128:20–21)—are here on earth to bless humanity. As the capstone to the blessings of the gospel, the powers restored by Elias and Elijah enable us to organize and seal family units for time and all eternity and to make of earth a heaven and of man a god.

DOCTRINES OF CONSOLATION

Alvin Smith stands as an illustration of a great and supernal truth: Our Heavenly Father is eager to save as many of his children as will be saved. Moral agency is foundational in the great plan of happiness, and each son and daughter of God will have the opportunity, either here or hereafter, to receive the fulness of the gospel of Jesus Christ and participate in the covenants, ordinances, and blessings associated with exaltation in the celestial kingdom. "Now, what do we hear in the gospel which we have received? A voice of gladness! A voice

103

of mercy from heaven; and a voice of truth out of the earth; glad tidings for the dead; a voice of gladness for the living and the dead; glad tidings of great joy" (D&C 128:19). The sacred doctrines of salvation, including the transcendent truths associated with the redemption of men and women on both sides of the veil of death, have come to us "line upon line, precept upon precept; here a little and there a little; giving us consolation by holding forth that which is to come, confirming our hope!" (D&C 128:21.) We will now speak briefly about some of those doctrines of consolation.

The eternal family. Ultimate salvation is found only in the eternal union of man and woman. Every priesthood, grace, power, and authority restored to the Prophet Joseph Smith centers on the salvation of the family. Peter, James, and John restored the Holy Priesthood, thereby authorizing men to perform the ordinances of salvation; Elias restored the ordinances of eternal marriage and the promise of an endless seed; and Elijah restored the sealing power and the fulness of the priesthood by which husband, wife, and children are bound eternally. These doctrines build on the assurance of the Book of Mormon that the resurrection is corporeal and thus that women will be resurrected as women and men as men, the bond of their love ever intact. They in turn must be bound in eternal covenant with their righteous progenitors and their posterity. In that eternal and restored system we know as Mormonism, salvation is a family affair.

Why would God create us male and female, command that a man leave his father and mother and cleave unto his wife and none else, only to have the couple separated forevermore in death, never again to be united? Yet such are the solemn beliefs of many; they teach that in heaven the righteous will be involved in an everlasting liturgy of praise to God or an endless meditation in solitude of his divine majesty and goodness, having no eternal interest in those who were so important to them here. The earth, according to such notions, being in all its dimensions deficient to the order of heaven, is to be destroyed along with our memory of all earthly associations.

Many Christians, anxious to be true to biblical teachings, find themselves in a dilemma when it comes to speaking of the continuation of the marital union and the family beyond the grave. It just seems natural and right and appropriate to think of being forever with someone they love. And yet they read the New Testament and find Jesus explaining that "in the resurrection they neither marry nor are given in marriage" (Matthew 22:30). Note the following commentaries on the misunderstood passage from Matthew:

"God is able to transform us into creatures who do not engage in sexual relations or procreate. . . . Lack of sex or marriage does not in any way diminish heavenly bliss. In the life to come, all interpersonal relationships will no doubt far surpass the most intimate and pleasurable of human intercourse as we now know it. Neither jealousy nor exclusivism will mar human interaction in any way."[9]

"Had they [the Sadducees] recognized the power of God, they would have understood that God is able to raise the dead in such a manner that marriage will no longer be needed. . . . The glorious resurrected body . . . is going to be immortal. Since there will be no death, the race will not have to be reproduced. Marriage, accordingly, will be a matter of the past."[10]

"The question I'm most often asked about heaven is, 'Will I be married to the same spouse in heaven?' Most are saying, 'I don't want to lose my relationship with my wife; I can't imagine going to heaven and not being married to her.' . . .

"Marriage and other business of this life can sometimes intrude on more important matters of eternal concern. Paul writes, 'He that is unmarried careth for the things that belong to the Lord, how he may please the Lord: but he that is married careth for the things that are of the world, how he may please his wife' (1 Cor. 7:32–33). So if you can remain single, do. Concentrate on the things of the Lord, because marriage is only a temporary provision. . . .

"Jesus' reply [to the Sadducees] was a sharp rebuke for their ignorance of the Scriptures: 'Ye do err, not knowing the scriptures, nor the power of God. For in the resurrection they neither marry, nor are given in marriage, but are as the angels of God in heaven' (vv. 29–30).

"In other words, angels don't procreate. Neither will we in heaven. All the reasons for marriage will be gone. Here on earth man needs a helper, woman needs a protector, and God has designed both to produce children. In heaven, man will no longer require a helper because he will be perfect. Woman will no longer need a protector because she will be perfect. And the population of heaven will be fixed. Thus marriage as an institution will be unnecessary. . . .

"But what are those of us who are happily married supposed to think of this? I love my wife. She's my best friend and my dearest companion in every area of life. If those are your thoughts about your spouse as well, don't despair! You will enjoy an eternal companionship in heaven that is more perfect than any earthly partnership. The difference is that you will have such a perfect relationship with every other person in heaven as well. If having such a deep relationship with your spouse here is so wonderful, imagine how glorious it will be to enjoy a perfect relationship with every human in the whole expanse of heaven—forever!"[11]

What did the Savior mean when he spoke to the Sadducees? To properly understand the disputed scriptural passage, we must ask, To whom was the statement of the Savior directed? Clearly he was addressing himself to the Sadducees, a Jewish sect who denied life after death, the resurrection of the body, angels, or spirits. In addition, they obviously rejected Jesus the Messiah and his gospel and considered the Lord to be a threat to their craft and their influence among the people. In a broader sense, the text applies to all who reject the gospel and the power and authority to act in the name of God. None such can claim a sealing bond between marriage partners beyond the grave.

The modern equivalent is for a person who does not accept the restored gospel or our belief in resurrection or the afterlife to ask the president of the Church which of the seven men she had been married to (in civil ceremonies) would be hers in the world to come. The answer, of course, is none of them. Because one unbeliever has been told that her civil marriages are not binding in eternity and thus that her spouses and children cannot be secured hereafter is not to say that that is true for everyone else, especially for those whose marriages are solemnized in holy temples by proper authority. "For that matter," Elder Bruce R. McConkie taught, "there is no revelation, either ancient or modern, which says there is neither marrying nor giving in marriage in heaven itself for righteous people. All that the revelations set forth is that such is denied to the Sadducees and other worldly and ungodly people."[12] Nor does the New Testament passage justify the idea that resurrected beings cannot be married or that other gospel ordinances cannot be performed for people after they have been resurrected.

The following statement from a modern apostle of the Lord Jesus Christ, Elder Parley P. Pratt, represents a marvelous contrast to the commentaries quoted above:

"It was at this time [in Philadelphia in 1839] that I received from [Joseph Smith] the first idea of eternal family organization, and the eternal union of the sexes in those inexpressibly endearing relationships which none but the highly intellectual, the refined and pure in heart, know how to prize, and which are at the very foundation of everything worthy to be called happiness.

"Till then I had learned to esteem kindred affections and sympathies as appertaining solely to this transitory state, as something from which the heart must be entirely weaned, in order to be fitted for its heavenly state.

"It was Joseph Smith who taught me how to prize the endearing relationships of father and mother, husband and wife; of brother and sister, son and daughter.

"It was from him that I learned that the wife of my bosom might be secured to me for time and all eternity; and that the refined sympathies and affections which endeared us to each other emanated from the fountain of divine eternal love. It was from him that I learned that we might cultivate these affections, and grow and increase in the same to all eternity. . . .

"I had loved before, but I knew not why. But now I loved—with a pureness—an intensity of elevated, exalted feeling, which would lift my soul from the transitory things of this groveling sphere and expand it as the ocean. I felt that God was my heavenly Father indeed; that Jesus was my brother, and that the wife of my bosom was an immortal, eternal companion; a kind ministering angel, given to me as a comfort, and a crown of glory for ever and ever. In short, I could now love with the spirit and with the understanding also."[13]

Many of earth's inhabitants, including many of the household of faith who are worthy in every other way, will not have the opportunity to marry in the temple. What will become of them? What of those who deeply and dearly desired to enjoy all of the privileges and sweet blessings associated with the eternal family unit but never were afforded that opportunity? President Lorenzo Snow taught: "There is no Latter-day Saint who dies after having lived a faithful life who will lose anything because of having failed to do certain things when opportunities were not furnished him or her. In other words, if a young man or a young woman has no opportunity of getting married, and they live faithful lives up to the time of their death, they will have all the blessings, exaltation, and glory that any man or woman will have who had this opportunity and improved it. That is sure and positive."[14]

The family is the most important unit in time and in eternity, and no organization, even such divinely revealed ones as the Church and its auxiliaries, should take priority over the family. Because the family is so central to the great plan of happiness, our Heavenly Father has made provision for its everlasting perpetuation. That provision is eternal marriage and the sealing of husband and wife, parents and children, through the sacred ordinances of the temple. The power to bind and seal, on earth and in heaven, that makes it all possible.

Securing the children. The Prophet Joseph Smith stated: "Our heavenly Father is more liberal in His views, and boundless in His mercies and blessings, than we are ready to believe or receive."[15] In speaking at the funeral for Judge Elias Higbee on 13 August 1843, the Prophet stated: "Had I inspiration, revelation, and lungs to communicate what my soul has contemplated in times past, there is not a soul in this congregation but would go to their homes and shut their mouths in everlasting silence on religion till they had learned something. Why be so certain that you comprehend the things of God, when all things with you are so uncertain. You are welcome to all the knowledge and intelligence I can impart to you." After thus preparing the Saints for what was to come, he continued: "That which hath been hid from before the foundation of the world is revealed to babes and sucklings in the last days. The world is reserved unto burning in the last days. He shall send Elijah the prophet, and he shall reveal the

109

covenants of the fathers in relation to the children, and the covenants of the children in relation to the fathers."

He then referred to the four angels of Revelation 7, described in modern revelation as "four angels sent forth from God, to whom is given power over the four parts of the earth, to save life and to destroy; these are they who have the everlasting gospel to commit to every nation, kindred, tongue, and people; having power to shut up the heavens, to seal up unto life, or to cast down to the regions of darkness" (D&C 77:8). The Prophet declared: "Four destroying angels holding power over the four quarters of the earth until the servants of God are sealed in their foreheads, which signifies sealing the blessing upon their heads, meaning the everlasting covenant, thereby making their calling and election sure. When a seal is put upon the father and mother, it secures their posterity, so that they cannot be lost, but will be saved by virtue of the covenant of their father and mother."[16]

Only a moment's reflection on these words draws forth the question: To what degree can righteous parents, fathers and mothers who have entered into and kept sacred covenants, affect and effect the salvation of their posterity? President Brigham Young taught: "Let the father and mother, who are members of this Church and kingdom, take a righteous course, and strive with all their might never to do a wrong, but to do good all their lives; if they have one child or one hundred children, if they conduct themselves towards them as they should, binding them to the Lord by their faith and prayers, I care not where those children go, they are bound up to their parents by an everlasting tie, and no power on earth or hell can separate them from their parents in eternity; they will return again to the fountain from whence they sprang."[17]

We believe that those who are faithful in their first estate come to the earth with certain predispositions to receive and

110

embrace the truth. The Prophet Joseph himself declared that those of the house of Israel who come into the Church do so with quiet receptivity to the Spirit of the Lord and an openness to pure intelligence.[18] Similarly, we have no difficulty speaking of the Spirit of Elijah in reaching out, touching, directing, and impelling individuals to search out their dead and perform the saving ordinances. Why should we have difficulty accepting the truth that the power of the covenant can and will reach out, touch, redirect, and impel wandering sheep? Could it be that that power is indeed the same Spirit of Elijah, the Spirit that turns the hearts of the children to the covenant made with their fathers?

Elder Orson F. Whitney offered the following powerful commentary on Joseph Smith's words: "The Prophet Joseph Smith declared—and he never taught more comforting doctrine—that the eternal sealings of faithful parents and the divine promises made to them for valiant service in the cause of truth, would save not only themselves but likewise their posterity. Though some of the sheep may wander, the eye of the shepherd is upon them, and sooner or later they will feel the tentacles of divine providence reaching out after them and drawing them back to the fold. Either in this life or in the life to come, they will return. They will have to pay their debt to justice; they will suffer for their sins; and may tread a thorny path; but if it leads them at last, like the penitent prodigal, to a loving and forgiving father's heart and home, the painful experience will not have been in vain. Pray for your careless and disobedient children; hold on to them with your faith. Hope on, trust on, till you see the salvation of God. . . .

"You parents of the wilful and the wayward: Don't give them up. Don't cast them off. They are not utterly lost. The shepherd will find his sheep. They were his before they were yours—long before he entrusted them to your care; and you cannot begin to love them as he loves them. They have but strayed in ignorance from the Path of Right, and God is merciful to ignorance. Only the fulness of knowledge brings the fulness of accountability. Our Heavenly Father is far more merciful, infinitely more charitable, than even the best of his servants, and the Everlasting Gospel is mightier in power to save than our narrow finite minds can comprehend."[19]

In our own day, Elder Boyd K. Packer has provided a comforting context and reaffirmation for the promise to faithful parents. In discussing the moral pollution of the last days, he said: "It is a great challenge to raise a family in the darkening mists of our moral environment. We emphasize that the greatest work you will do will be within the walls of your home [Harold B. Lee, Conference Report, April 1973, 130], and that 'no other success can compensate for failure in the home' [David O. McKay, Conference Report, April 1935, 116]. The measure of our success as parents, however, will not rest solely on how our children turn out. That judgment would be just only if we could raise our families in a perfectly moral environment, and that now is not possible.

"It is not uncommon for responsible parents to lose one of their children, for a time, to influences over which they have no control. They agonize over rebellious sons and daughters. They are puzzled over why they are so helpless when they have tried so hard to do what they should. It is my conviction that those wicked influences one day will be overruled. . . .

"We cannot overemphasize the value of temple marriage, the binding ties of the sealing ordinance, and the standards of worthiness required of them. When parents keep the covenants they have made at the altar of the temple, their children will be forever bound to them."[20]

We all know that even a merciful God will not violate an individual's moral agency, that he will force no man to heaven. Exaltation in the celestial kingdom is reserved for those who choose to go there, not those who were coerced or manipulated into appropriate behavior. We know that the laws of the everlasting covenant cannot violate the principles of justice or the canons of right and wrong. And yet there seems to be, in the sermons and writings of the prophets, the quiet but soul-satisfying message that the alms of the prayers of the righteous do come up into the ears of the Lord of Sabaoth; that righteous parents' loyalty to their covenants will not be overlooked; that no amount of suffering of the faithful in behalf of their posterity will be for naught; and that there is power, remarkable power in the covenant, to save those who will be saved. President Joseph Fielding Smith taught: "Those born under the covenant, throughout all eternity, are the children of their parents. Nothing except the unpardonable sin, or sin unto death, can break this tie. If children do not sin as John says [1 John 5:16–17], 'unto death,' the parents may still feel after them and eventually bring them back to them again."[21] As Elder Packer suggested, it may be that the oppressive power of evil in these last days is such that it chokes or restrains the proper exercise of agency. One day that will change.

But doesn't the Prophet Joseph Smith's statement regarding the sealing of righteous parents indicate that the parents' calling and election must be made sure? It certainly sounds that way. We must, however, keep some other points in mind. Latter-day Saints who have received the ordinances of salvation—including the blessings of the temple endowment and eternal marriage—may thus press forward in the work of the Lord and with quiet dignity and patient maturity seek to be worthy of gaining the certain assurance of salvation before the end of their mortal lives. But should one not formally receive that more sure word of prophecy in this life, he has the scriptural promise that faithfully enduring to the end—keeping the covenants and commandments from baptism to the end of his life (Mosiah 18:8–9)—eventuates in the promise of eternal life, whether that promise be received here or hereafter (D&C 14:7; 53:7; see also 2 Nephi 31:20; Mosiah 5:15). "But blessed are they who are faithful and endure, whether in life or in death, for they shall inherit eternal life" (D&C 50:5).

Elder Bruce R. McConkie expressed the following sentiments at the funeral of Elder S. Dilworth Young: "If we die in the faith, that is the same thing as saying that our calling and election has been made sure and that we will go on to eternal reward hereafter. As far as faithful members of the Church are concerned, they have charted a course leading to eternal life. This life is the time that is appointed as a probationary estate for men to prepare to meet God, and as far as faithful people are concerned, if they are in the line of their duty, if they are doing what they ought to do, although they may not have been perfect in this sphere, their probation is ended. Now there will be some probation for some other people hereafter. But for the faithful saints of God, now is the time and the day, and their probation is ended with their death."[22]

The pull of the covenant toward righteousness may come from both sides of the veil. The counsel of Elisha the prophet is still timely: "Fear not: for they that be with us are more than they that be with them" (2 Kings 6:16). President Joseph F. Smith, in a conference address in April 1916 entitled "In the Presence of the Divine," made the following impressive and instructive remarks:

"Sometimes the Lord expands our vision from this point of view and this side of the veil, so that we feel and seem to realize that we can look beyond the thin veil which separates us from that other sphere. If we can see, by the enlightening influence of the Spirit of God and through the words that have been spoken by the holy prophets of God, beyond the veil that separates us from the spirit world, surely those who have passed beyond, can see more clearly through the veil back here to us than it is possible for us to see to them from our sphere of action. I believe we move and have our being in the presence of heavenly messengers and of heavenly beings. We are not separate from them. We begin to realize, more and more fully, as we become acquainted with the principles of the gospel, as they have been revealed anew in this dispensation, that we are closely related to our kindred, to our ancestors, to our friends and associates and co-laborers who have preceded us into the spirit world. We can not forget them; we do not cease to love them; we always hold them in our hearts, in memory. . . . How much more certain it is and reasonable and consistent to believe that those who have been faithful, who have gone beyond and are still engaged in the work for the salvation of the souls of men, . . . can see us better than we can see them; that they know us better than we know them. They have advanced; we are advancing; we are growing as they have grown; we are reaching the goal that they have attained unto; and therefore, I claim that we live in their presence, they see us, they are solicitous for our welfare, they love us now more than ever. For now they see the dangers that beset us; they can comprehend, better than ever before, the weaknesses that are liable to mislead us into dark and forbidden paths. They see the temptations and the evils that beset us in life and the proneness of mortal beings to yield to temptation and to wrong doing; hence their solicitude for us, and their love for us, and their desire for our well being, must be greater than that which we feel for ourselves."[23]

We can make it. Do Latter-day Saints believe that men and women may only enjoy the benefits of salvation in the world to come? Is there no sense in which we may be saved in the present, in the here and now? Though we quickly acknowledge that most scriptural references to salvation seem to point toward that which comes in the next life, we do have within our theology principles and doctrines that suggest a form of salvation in this life. Perhaps the most obvious illustration is

115

when a member of the Church makes his or her calling and election sure. As Joseph Smith taught, when we exercise saving faith and demonstrate our willingness to serve God at all hazards, we eventually, in this life or the next (D&C 14:7; 50:5; 58:2), receive the assurance of eternal life.[24]

If the more sure word of prophecy, the knowledge that we are sealed up unto eternal life (D&C 131:5), comes to us in this life, then our salvation is secure, or we might say, fairly secure. In fact, there is never a time in this life when faithful endurance to the end is not required. The scriptures teach that a man or woman may fall from grace and depart from the living God; that even the sanctified must take heed lest they fall (D&C 20:30–34;124:124); that those who were once enlightened and have tasted the heavenly gift may fall away (Hebrews 6:4–6). Those who have been sealed to eternal life are no doubt fully aware that they must stay faithful to the end, but even so they know assuredly that if they were to die suddenly, their salvation is secure. Thus they are saved, or, to put it another way, they are living in a saved condition; there is a condition or state we may attain unto in this mortal life in which salvation hereafter is promised here; the day of judgment has essentially been advanced.

But is there any way to know we are saved other than receiving the more sure word of prophecy? The prophets seem to suggest that there is. The same Holy Spirit of Promise that searches the hearts of men and women, that ratifies and approves and seals ordinances and lives, that same Holy Spirit serves, as Paul indicates, as the "earnest of our inheritance" (Ephesians 1:14). The Lord's "earnest money" on us, his down payment, his indication to us that he fully intends to save us, is the Holy Spirit. We know that we are on course when the Spirit is with us. We know that our lives are approved of God when the Spirit is with us. We know that we are in Christ, in covenant, when the Spirit is with us. And we know that we are saved when the Spirit is with us. If we live in such a way that we can partake of the sacrament worthily, hold and use a current temple recommend, and maintain the gift and gifts of the Spirit, then we are in the line of our duty; we are approved of the heavens, and if we were to die suddenly, we would go into paradise and eventually into the celestial kingdom.

A modern revelation attests: "But learn that he who doeth the works of righteousness shall receive his reward, even peace in this world, and eternal life in the world to come" (D&C 59:23). Indeed, we might liken the words of the Lord to Oliver Cowdery to ourselves: "If you desire a further witness, cast your mind upon the night that you cried unto me in your heart, that you might know concerning the truth of these things. Did I not speak peace to your mind? What greater witness can you have than from God?" (D&C 6:22–23). We are living in a saved condition to the extent that we are living in the light, living according to our spiritual privileges, living in harmony with the knowledge and the blessings we have received to that point. The following is an intriguing statement from President Brigham Young:

"If a person with an honest heart, a broken, contrite, and pure spirit, in all fervency and honesty of soul, presents himself and says that he wishes to be baptized for the remission of his sins, and the ordinance is administered by one having authority, is that man saved? Yes, to that period of time. Should the Lord see proper to take him then from the earth, the man has believed and been baptized, and is a fit subject for heaven—a candidate for the kingdom of God in the celestial world, because he has repented and done all that was required of him at that hour. . . .

"It is present salvation and the present influence of the Holy Ghost that we need every day to keep us on saving ground. When an individual refuses to comply with the further requirements of heaven, then the sins he had formerly committed return upon his head; his former righteousness departs from him, and is not accounted to him for righteousness: but if he had continued in righteousness and obedience to the requirements of heaven, he is saved all the time, through baptism, the laying on of hands, and obeying the commandments of the Lord and all that is required of him by the heavens—the living oracles. He is saved now, next week, next year, and continually, and is prepared for the celestial kingdom of God whenever the time comes for him to inherit it.

"I want present salvation. I preach, comparatively, but little about the eternities and Gods, and their wonderful works in eternity; and do not tell who first made them, nor how they were made; for I know nothing about that. Life is for us, and it is for us to receive it today, and not wait for the Millennium. Let us take a course to be saved today, and, when evening comes, review the acts of the day, repent of our sins, if we have any to repent of, and say our prayers; then we can lie down and sleep in peace until the morning, arise with gratitude to God, commence the labors of another day, and strive to live the whole day to God and nobody else."[25] Or, as President David O. McKay pointed out, "The gospel of Jesus Christ, as revealed to the Prophet Joseph Smith, is in very deed, in every way, the power of God unto salvation. It is salvation *here*—here and now. It gives to every man the perfect life, here and now, as well as hereafter."[26]

"I am in the hands of the Lord," President Young pointed out, "and never trouble myself about my salvation, or what the Lord will do with me hereafter."[27] As he said on another occasion, our work "is a work of the present. The salvation we are seeking is for the present, and sought correctly, it can be obtained, and be continually enjoyed. If it continues today, it is upon the same principle that it will continue tomorrow, the next day, the next week, or the next year, and, we might say, the next eternity."[28]

Though we must guard against all forms of pride or self-assurance, we must also avoid the kind of false modesty or doubt that is antithetical to faith. As Joseph Smith taught, doubt—certainly including a constant worry as to our standing before God or our capacity to go where Christ is—cannot coexist with saving faith. Fear and doubt "preclude the possibility of the exercise of faith in [God] for life and salvation."[29] If indeed "happiness is the object and design of our existence,"[30] then happiness is something to be enjoyed in the present, in the here and now, not something reserved for the distant there and then. "If we are saved," President Young declared, "we are happy, we are filled with light, glory, intelligence, and we pursue a course to enjoy the blessings that the Lord has in store for us. If we continue to pursue that course, it produces just the thing we want, that is, to be saved at this present moment. And that will lay the foundation to be saved forever and forever, which will amount to an eternal salvation."[31]

Living in a state of salvation does not entail an inordinate self-confidence but rather a hope in Christ. To hope in our modern world is to wish, to worry, to fret about some particular outcome. In the scriptures, however, hope is expectation, anticipation, and assurance. Faith in Christ, true faith, always gives rise to hope in Christ. "And what is it that ye shall hope for? Behold I say unto you that ye shall have hope through the atonement of Christ and the power of his resurrection, to be raised unto life eternal" (Moroni 7:41). To have faith in Christ is to have the assurance that as we rely wholly upon his merits and mercy and trust in his redeeming grace, we will make it (2 Nephi 31:19; Moroni 6:4). Not only will he bridge the chasm between the ideal and the real and thus provide that final spiritual boost into eternal life but he will also

119

extend to us that marvelous enabling power so essential to daily living, a power that enables us to conquer weakness and acquire the divine nature. In short, living in a state of salvation is living in the quiet assurance that God is in his heaven, Christ is the Lord, and the plan of redemption is real and in active operation in our individual lives. It is not to be totally free of weakness but to proceed confidently in the Savior's promise that in him we shall find strength to overcome, as well as rest and peace, here and hereafter.

CONCLUSION

Some things simply matter more than others. The family is the most important unit in time or in eternity, and no association, arrangement, or attachment can or should take precedence over it. Satan and his minions are busily at work in our day attempting to discredit, dismember, and displace the family. The Saints of the Most High God are under sacred covenant to be a light to a darkened world and as salt to a society whose excessive tolerance and misplaced loyalties have cost them dearly, including the near loss of the nuclear family. Latter-day prophets have stood boldly in defense of the family, and God has restored powers and keys that bind and seal those families everlastingly. In addition, we have the assurance that there is supernal power in the new and everlasting covenant, power to make a man and a woman as one, power to guide and return the wandering sheep to the fold and thereby heal and renew the family.

One of the great needs in our day is for us as Latter-day Saints to have balance in our lives, balance between zeal in keeping the commandments and patience in achieving our goals, balance between a wholehearted devotion to truth and a loving acceptance of those (including ourselves) who fall short. And in our individual lives there needs to be a balance between a type of divine discontent, in which we are

120

constantly striving to be better than we are, and what Nephi called a "perfect brightness of hope" (2 Nephi 31:20), the quiet but soul-affirming anticipation that if we trust in the Lord and seek earnestly to do our best, he will make up the difference in time and in eternity.

NOTES

1. "The Bible: A Sealed Book," in *Doctrines of the Restoration*, comp. Mark L. McConkie (Salt Lake City: Bookcraft, 1989), 292–93; see also Joseph Fielding Smith, *Doctrines of Salvation*, comp. Bruce R. McConkie, 3 vols. (Salt Lake City: Bookcraft, 1954–56), 3:85.

2. Bruce R. McConkie, *The Millennial Messiah: The Second Coming of the Son of Man* (Salt Lake City: Deseret Book, 1982), 264.

3. Joseph Smith, *Teachings of the Prophet Joseph Smith*, sel. Joseph Fielding Smith (Salt Lake City: Deseret Book, 1976), 337.

4. See Smith, *Teachings of the Prophet Joseph Smith*, 322.

5. Smith, *Teachings of the Prophet Joseph Smith*, 338.

6. See Smith, *Teachings of the Prophet Joseph Smith*, 172; see also Smith, *Doctrines of Salvation*, 2:115–28.

7. "What I Hope You Will Teach Your Children about the Temple," *Ensign*, August 1985, 10; emphasis in original.

8. James E. Faust, Conference Report, April 1993, 47.

9. Craig L. Blomberg, *The New American Commentary: Matthew* (Nashville, Tenn.: Broadman Press, 1992), 333.

10. William Hendriksen, *New Testament Commentary: Matthew* (Grand Rapids, Mich.: Baker Book House, 1973), 805–6.

11. John F. MacArthur, *The Glory of Heaven* (Wheaton, Ill.: Crossway Books, 1996), 134–38.

12. Bruce R. McConkie, *Doctrinal New Testament Commentary*, 3 vols. (Salt Lake City: Bookcraft, 1965–73), 1:607.

13. Parley P. Pratt, *Autobiography of Parley P. Pratt* (Salt Lake City: Deseret Book, 1976), 297–98.

14. Lorenzo Snow, *Teachings of Lorenzo Snow*, comp. Clyde J. Williams (Salt Lake City: Bookcraft, 1984), 138.

15. Smith, *Teachings of the Prophet Joseph Smith*, 257.

16. Smith, *Teachings of the Prophet Joseph Smith*, 321.

17. Brigham Young, *Journal of Discourses*, 26 vols. (London: Latter-day Saints' Book Depot, 1851–86), 11:215.

18. Smith, *Teachings of the Prophet Joseph Smith*, 149–50.

19. Orson F. Whitney, Conference Report, April 1929, 110.

20. Boyd K. Packer, Conference Report, April 1992, 94–95.

21. Smith, *Doctrines of Salvation*, 2:90.

22. Bruce R. McConkie, address at funeral service for S. Dilworth Young, 13 July 1981, typescript, 5.

23. *Messages of the First Presidency of The Church of Jesus Christ of Latter-day Saints,* comp. James R. Clark, 6 vols. (Salt Lake City: Bookcraft, 1965–75), 5:6–7.
24. Smith, *Teachings of the Prophet Joseph Smith,* 150.
25. Brigham Young, *Journal of Discourses,* 8:124–25.
26. David O. McKay, *Gospel Ideals* (Salt Lake City: The Improvement Era, 1953), 6.
27. Brigham Young, *Journal of Discourses,* 6:276.
28. Brigham Young, *Journal of Discourses,* 1:31.
29. Joseph Smith, *Lectures on Faith* (Salt Lake City: Deseret Book, 1985), 4:13; see also 3:20–21; 6:12.
30. Smith, *Teachings of the Prophet Joseph Smith,* 255.
31. Brigham Young, *Journal of Discourses,* 1:31.

Epilogue

I sat beside my father only hours before his death. He knew, and I knew, that a chapter in his eternal journey was coming to a close. There was a yearning in my soul to communicate—no, to commune—about sacred things, about things that matter most. We spoke at length about home and family and temples and covenants and sealings and eternal life. We expressed our love to each other and brought to an end, at least for a short season, a sweet association, one that I look forward to resuming more than I can say.

I knew that I would miss him, that our family, especially my mother, would mourn his loss and that it would be impossible to completely fill the void of his passing. And yet there was no doubt whatsoever, in his heart or mine, that Albert Louis Millet would continue to live, that he was about to be transferred to another field of labor. I was totally at peace during those tender moments, and that consummate assurance continued through his death and funeral. It continues to this day, after more than a decade. It is a peace born of perspective, a peace undergirded by the restored doctrine of life after death. It is a peace which derives from that Spirit who confirms that what my father taught me through the years about life after death is indeed true.

Since that time I have on several occasions held the hand

of those who stared death in the face, those sanctified souls whose lives equipped them to avoid the sting of death and almost seemed to rob the grim reaper of his victory. Our doctrine informs. It inspires. It empowers. Although we may not possess the answers to all of life's hard questions, we do have a surprising number of answers. And those answers testify of the reality of the postmortal spirit world; of the eternal verity that there are more kingdoms than one in the world to come; that our gracious Lord has made provision for men and women to learn of him—to learn of his gospel and of his great plan of happiness—either here or hereafter; that the ordinances of salvation, those sacred rites that serve as channels of divine power and are thus necessary for the fulness of eternal reward hereafter, may be received in temples by mortals in behalf of those who have passed beyond the veil of death; that life and love and learning and growth and expansion continue in the postmortal spirit world, all in preparation for the glorious resurrection; and that there is power in the gospel covenant, power to unite and bind husband and wife, parents and children, in an eternal unit that spans the veil.

We believe the scriptures. We believe that the doctrine of life after death is neither myth nor metaphor, that the burden of holy writ is that we can exercise a lively hope in what lies ahead. Our identities continue. The resurrected body is a physical, tangible reality. The continuation of families and the resumption of valued associations are real. Truly, as the Prophet Joseph Smith declared, "that same sociality which exists among us here will exist among us there, only it will be coupled with eternal glory, which glory we do not now enjoy" (D&C 130:2).

Unlike so many others in the religious world, the Latter-day Saints anticipate celestial life on a material world. Elder Orson Pratt eloquently declared: "A Saint who is one in deed and truth, does not look for an immaterial heaven, but he

124

expects a heaven with lands, houses, cities, vegetation, rivers, and animals; with thrones, temples, palaces, kings, princes, priests, and angels; with food, raiment, musical instruments, etc., all of which are material. Indeed, the Saints' eternal home is a redeemed, glorified, celestial material creation, inhabited by glorified material beings, male and female, organized into families, embracing all the relationships of husbands and wives, parents and children, where sorrow, crying, pain, and death will be known no more." On this earth, Elder Pratt continued, the Saints of God "expect to live, with body, parts, and holy passions; on it they expect to move and have their being." In short, "materiality is indelibly stamped upon the very heaven of heavens, upon all the eternal creations; it is the very essence of all existence."[1]

I bear witness that Jesus is the Christ, the Savior and Redeemer of our souls. He has "abolished death, and hath brought life and immortality to light through the gospel" (2 Timothy 1:10). Immortality comes to each of us as a free gift because of who Christ is. Eternal life, the greatest of all the gifts of God (D&C 6:13; 14:7), is made available to us because of what he has done. "As mortals we all must die," President Gordon B. Hinckley explained. "Death is as much a part of eternal life as is birth. Looked at through mortal eyes, without comprehension of the eternal plan of God, death is a bleak, final, and unrelenting experience. . . .

"But our Eternal Father, whose children we are, made possible a far better thing through the sacrifice of His Only Begotten Son, the Lord Jesus Christ. This had to be. Can anyone believe that the Great Creator would provide for life and growth and achievement only to snuff it all into oblivion in the process of death? Reason says no. Justice demands a better answer. The God of heaven has given one. The Lord Jesus Christ provided it."[2]

I bear further witness that Joseph Smith, the Choice Seer,

was called by God and empowered to restore the everlasting gospel to the earth, including those singular truths associated with the immortality of the human soul. The Church of Jesus Christ of Latter-day Saints is the custodian of the fulness of the gospel of Jesus Christ, is the kingdom of God on earth, and, as now constituted under the direction of living apostles and prophets, is preparing a people for the second coming of the Son of Man and for eternal glory in the worlds to come. God grant that we might appreciate what we have been given and thus live in such a way as to qualify for the highest of eternal rewards when we are called upon to pass through death into life hereafter.

NOTES

1. Orson Pratt, *Masterful Discourses and Writings of Orson Pratt*, comp. N. B. Lundwall (Salt Lake City: Bookcraft, 1962), 62–63.
2. Gordon B. Hinckley, *Teachings of Gordon B. Hinckley* (Salt Lake City: Deseret Book, 1997), 152.

Index